Rosalie Haffner-Lee Zinke

Pacific Press® Publishing Association
Nampa, Idaho
Oshawa, Ontario, Canada
www.pacificpress.com

Cover design by Gerald Lee Monks
Cover design resources from Lars Justinen
Inside design by Aaron Troia

You can obtain additional copies of this book by calling toll-free 1-800-765-6955 or by visiting http://www.adventistbookcenter.com.

Library of Congress Cataloging-in-Publication Data:

Zinke, Rosalie Haffner-Lee, 1931-
Worship / Rosalie Haffner-Lee Zinke.
p. cm.
ISBN 13: 978-0-8163-2451-4
ISBN 10: 0-8163-2451-4
1. Worship—Biblical teaching. I. Title.
BS680.W78Z56 2011
264—dc22

2010044086

11 12 13 14 15 • 5 4 3 2 1

Dedication

To my husband, Dave, and other family members who lovingly encouraged and supported me during the writing of this book. And to Lorraine Hansen, who spent many hours formatting and editing this manuscript.

Other books by
Rosalie Haffner-Lee Zinke:

Let Me Tell You About My God: The Psalms Portray God

Never Far From Grace: First and Second Samuel

Contents

Introduction

As you open this book, a bit of background may be helpful. The little parable that follows is based on 2 Corinthians 4:7, NLT. "We now have this light shining in our hearts, but we ourselves are like *fragile clay jars* containing this great treasure" (emphasis supplied).

Rose, a fragile clay jar, had retired from active duty for the third time when she felt impressed to begin a study of Scripture to better understand what God says about worship. A crisis over worship had led this jar to do some heart-searching: *Why should the worship of God cause conflict in the church? What should or should not happen in worship? Do I really know how to properly worship God?* In answer, a still, small Voice seemed to say, "If you want to know how to worship, read My instruction manual!"

By the time the jar completed her study of the first two books of the Bible, Genesis and Exodus, her excitement about what she was learning there regarding worship led the jar to speak with other clay jars—jars who had great biblical experience and wisdom. They suggested she write some Bible study guides on worship. The jar had experience in writing study guides and knew how much work is involved in such a project.

"I'm retired; I don't need or want another job! However, Lord, if this really is what You want me to do—well, I'll pray about it, and You can let me know!" The Lord has His ways, and the study guides began to take shape. About halfway through the project, the clay jar began to think about her own inadequate worship.

Here I am, learning all these profound concepts about worship and writing about them, but is my own worship experience really what it should be?

Sitting at her desk one day, the clay jar pondered the dilemma. An inaudible Voice said emphatically, "Read *Selected Messages,* book one, page three hundred forty-four." Immediately, the jar knew what was on that page. This favorite quote was underlined and had been used many times. Yet somehow, its application to worship had never quite clicked. Suddenly, a light turned on—the light of the glory of God in the face of Jesus Christ. The months of intense study and writing began to take on a whole new meaning in the light of this passage:

> The religious services, the prayers, the praise, the penitent confession of sin [all acts of worship] ascend from true believers as incense to the heavenly sanctuary, but passing through the corrupt channels of humanity, they are so defiled that unless purified by blood, they can never be of value with God. . . . All incense from earthly tabernacles must be moist with the cleansing drops of the blood of Christ. . . . He gathers into . . . [His] censer the prayers, the praise, and the confessions of His people, and with these He puts His own spotless righteousness. Then . . . the incense comes up before God wholly and entirely acceptable. . . . Oh, that all may see that everything in obedience, in penitence, in praise and thanksgiving, must be placed upon the glowing fire of the righteousness of Christ. The fragrance of this righteousness ascends like a cloud around the mercy seat.[1]

Human "clay jars" are not capable of giving to God what He deserves in worship. So, Jesus offers up to His Father along with His own precious blood all that the clay jars give to God in worship—their obedience, praise, and thanksgiving, the dedication of their lives to Him, offerings, talents, and abilities. Jesus then adds to these sacrifices His own spotless righteousness! "Then, perfumed with the merits of Christ . . . the incense comes up before God wholly . . . acceptable."[2]

You, too, may realize that you are just a fragile clay jar, "containing this great treasure" (2 Corinthians 4:7, NLT). So as you walk through the pages of this book, may you read each chapter and understand it in the light of two great truths: 1. We are living in the last days of the great conflict between good and evil. As will be seen in the following chapters, worship—who to worship—is at the very heart of that great conflict. Shall we worship the Living God—God the Father and His Son,

Jesus Christ, the Creator God, who paid the ultimate price for our redemption? Or shall we worship the usurper who stops at nothing to steal from God the worship that belongs to Him alone? That conflict affects every area of our lives, so it should not surprise us that the enemy has a plan to counteract God's plan, especially in our worship of God.

When the writing of this book was nearing completion, the enemy was angry, and this clay jar, Rose, was struck with a serious illness. In spite of the setback and delay, the Lord gave strength to the clay jar to finish the project. God is still in control!

We will see, through this book, the conflict begin in the Garden of Eden and continue throughout the history of God's people. And we will see it reach its final great and terrible climax in the closing chapters of the book of Revelation. To help us prepare for these last days of earth's history and to stand firm before our wonderful God, especially in our worship of Him, is the objective and purpose of the pages you are about to read.

2. In the light of this conflict, it is well for us to see worship in perhaps a new light. As we have seen, the best we have to give to God in worship is inadequate because it comes from our sinful humanity. However, when we do give Him the best we have in our worship—coming from hearts that love and adore Him, and want more than anything else to please Him—we will then begin to see worship in a new light. Only His intercession can make our best acceptable as it comes up before the throne of God, beautiful and fragrant with the incense of the righteousness of Christ our Savior, acceptable because of our Great High Priest and Intercessor! Praise the Lord!

The objective of every page of this book is to point us to the source of our spiritual life—the righteousness of Jesus Christ—as we worship Him, our blessed Savior and Lord. To that end may every fragile clay jar be blessed with "the glory of God . . . in the face of Jesus Christ" because they contain "this great treasure" (2 Corinthians 4:6, 7, NLT)!

---

1. Ellen G. White, *Selected Messages* (Washington, D.C.: Review and Herald® Publishing Association, 1958), 1:344.

2. Ibid.

CHAPTER 1

The War Over Worship

The words *war* and *worship* seem to be a universe apart, yet the worship wars rage on in our postmodern society. Adventist theologian Karl Tsatalbasidis has written about the changes and developments that have taken place in the religious world regarding worship. In an article titled, "The Emerging Church: More Than Just a Facelift," he reviews the philosophies and trends that have affected worship in both Roman Catholic and Protestant churches, not excluding the Seventh-day Adventist Church. He reviews the classical era, which undergirds Roman Catholic theology then the modern era, which saw the Bible as culturally based, not divinely inspired and finally the postmodern era, characterized by the tearing down of the division between the sacred and the secular. "For emerging churches," he writes, "there are no longer any bad places, bad people, or bad times. All can be holy. All can be given to God in worship."[1] These philosophies opened the door to "anything you like." All is "OK for worship," including any kind of secular music. This was the beginning of the worship wars that ensued.

The beginning of the war over worship

The war over worship is not a new problem for the church. It began, in fact, in the courts of heaven when the divine Son of God, "through whom also He [God] made the worlds" (Hebrews 1:2) heard the Father say, " '*Let all the angels of God worship Him*' " (verse 6). God the Son had just spoken a brand-new planet into existence. " 'You, LORD, in the beginning laid the foundation of the earth' " (verse

10). He had created a perfect pair, Adam and Eve, to have dominion over all living things. They delighted in giving love, honor, and worship to their Creator.

Meanwhile in heaven, Lucifer, " ' " 'the anointed cherub' " ' " (Ezekiel 28:14) began harboring thoughts of self-exaltation. Why should the Son of God receive all the worship? Why should not he, as the highest angel, be entitled to the homage and worship given to the Creator? Those thoughts and feelings soon found utterance, as Lucifer spread his discontent caused by coveting the worship due to Christ alone. His desire for self-worship, fostered by pride and enhanced by his subtle deceptions, eventually erupted into open rebellion. What had appeared at first to be reverence for God, now became a crisis of whom to worship: Christ or Lucifer!

In the New Testament, Paul asserts, "By Him [Christ] all things were created that are in heaven and that are on earth. . . . All things were created through Him and for Him" (Colossians 1:16). He reminds us that just as surely as God spoke through the prophets, so now He has spoken through His Son "through whom also He made the worlds" (Hebrews 1:2). The Godhead claims the right to worship, because the Godhead created all things. This theme runs throughout Scripture and ends in the book of Revelation with the final call to planet Earth before Christ returns: " 'Fear God and give glory to Him, for the hour of His judgment has come; and *worship Him who made heaven and earth*' " (Revelation 14:7; emphasis supplied).

So from the very beginning of the conflict between Christ and Satan, the angels, one by one, had to choose to whom they would give their allegiance and worship. Because the Creator God is just and fair, and because He had given His created beings the power of choice, His newly created human family must now be given the option to choose whom they would worship—the Son of God, their Creator; or Lucifer, the fallen competitor who now vied for their worship.

Worship in Eden

The human, earthbound mind cannot begin to imagine the beauty of the original Garden home God created especially for the new pair. He covered them with garments of light, which reflected His holy character. Their Creator officiated at their marriage ceremony. Then He crowned His work by giving them a special day, the Sabbath, as a memorial of His creation, sanctified for all time as His day. The Sabbath was to be a constant reminder to the human family that He, the Creator, the Sovereign Ruler of the universe, is worthy of worship, reverence, and gratitude.

Crisis over worship

Then came the sad news of the crisis. Adam and Eve were warned not to go near the tree of the knowledge of good and evil. Their loyalty to God was to be tested. If they failed to follow God's counsel and yielded to the tempter, the result would be loss in the form of death. The test was one of loyalty to their Creator. Would they put Him first, worshiping and obeying Him at all costs? Or would they listen to the tempter and give their loyalty and worship to him?

The sad results are all too well known, for their choice that day has affected every member of the human family for every day that they live. Every human being must face the same choice that Adam and Eve faced that fateful day—the choice between worshiping their Creator or listening to the tempter and giving allegiance to him.

Their sin was not so much in believing the serpent's lie as it was distrusting the God who had given them life. The covering of light that had clothed them was now gone, and they were left with feelings of shame and guilt. Spiritual nakedness disqualifies human beings for the worship of God (see Revelation 3:16, 17). Even more painful than their guilt was the awful grief that now overwhelmed them as they realized their threefold loss—loss of innocence, loss of face-to-face communion with their Creator, and loss of their beautiful Garden home. Even the leaves falling from the trees caused a deeper grief in them than that which humans now feel for their dead.[2]

The Creator to the rescue

Adam and Eve had forfeited their right to live in the Garden of Eden, but the Son of God offered His own life to rescue the human family. Taking an innocent little lamb, perhaps a pet of Adam and Eve, God's Son took its life and then made them garments to cover their nakedness (see Genesis 3:21). He must have explained to them that their sin would cost the life of their Creator. Now they would worship Him not only as their Creator, but also as their Redeemer.

God promised, on that fateful day of their sin, that He would " 'put enmity between you [Satan] and the woman [God's people]' " (Genesis 3:15). He would send His own Son, the Creator, to do battle with the enemy, and though He would be bruised in the process, the Son would eventually win the battle over evil and sin. God's plan of salvation was explained to Adam and Eve; the sacrifice of His Son, symbolized by the dying lamb, was to give hope and consolation to the devastated couple. They were given a glimpse of the restoration of their Garden home and of the final victory of right over wrong. They were given rich promises to carry them through the difficult times that lay ahead!

A place of worship

God did one more thing to give them hope. Adam and Eve had worshiped God face-to-face in their Garden home. Now God gave them a new place where they could come to worship Him. Just outside the gate to the Garden of Eden, God's glory was revealed through the cherubim's flaming sword guarding the entrance (see Genesis 3:24). Here they and their descendants came to worship God, to renew their vows of loyalty to Him, and to offer their sacrifices as a token of their faith in His promise of salvation.[3] The same Hebrew word—*cherubim*—used here in Genesis 3:24 is also used in Exodus 25:17–20 to describe the cherubim covering the ark of the covenant with its *Shekinah* glory that represented the holy presence and glory of God in the Most Holy Place of the sanctuary. What a great God! Even though they had lost face-to-face communion with Him, He gave them this grand reminder of His glory!

Their grief over the loss of their Eden home was intense, but the promise of a Redeemer and the presence of the *Shekinah* glory at the Garden gate gave them courage and hope. God instructed them that they were to bring a sacrifice when they came to worship Him. The sacrifice, a lamb from their own flock, would be a symbol of what He would do for them someday; but it would also give them a way of expressing their appreciation to Him for what He had already done for them in the promise of a Redeemer—He had given them hope in place of despair!

Faith=obedience vs. Unbelief=rebellion

Adam and Eve brought their sons, Cain and Abel, to the gate of the Garden to worship through sacrifice. Each built an altar and offered his sacrifice; Abel bringing the required sacrifice of a lamb, while Cain brought the fruit he had harvested. He reasoned that his fruit was as good as a lamb. After all, what difference did it really make? Wasn't it more appropriate for him to bring fruit, since he himself had planted, cared for, and gathered it? Why should God be so particular? Besides, just the thought of taking an innocent lamb's life was most repulsive to him! He doubted God's wisdom in making such a big issue over his parents' first sin. In fact, in his heart there was a growing resentment against God; it seemed so unfair that they should be driven from the Garden over one small piece of fruit! The revolt of Lucifer was fomenting in Cain's heart. Suddenly, he was filled with anger against God, so he vented his feelings on his innocent brother, who had done no wrong to him! In that first murder, Abel became the victim of Cain's anger, and Cain became the father of the rebellious (see Genesis 4).

Two worshipers. Both came to worship. Both built altars. Both brought sacrifices. Both claimed to be worshiping God. God accepted one sacrifice but rejected the other. Was it the sacrifice itself that made the difference?

The slain lamb was a symbol of the One who would come and whose death for the sins of the human race alone could save them. Their parents had carefully explained to Cain and Abel that the wages of sin is death and that the sacrifice of the lamb demonstrated their faith in the ultimate Sacrifice to come. The fruit represented Cain's best efforts. However, no human effort can atone for sin. Only blood, the blood of the Lamb, can atone for sin. "By faith Abel offered to God a more excellent sacrifice than Cain" (Hebrews 11:4). Abel's faith resulted in obedience. Cain's unbelief drove him deeper into rebellion against God.

The story of Cain and Abel is a microcosm of the history of the human race. Two classes of worshipers. Two ways. Two destinies. Two different words are used to describe Cain and Abel's life work. The word used for Abel implies that he was a steward—that is, he managed what God had given him. The word used for Cain's occupation implies that he was in bondage to, or a worshiper of, the ground God gave him to care for.[4] Their posterity continued and will continue to exist until sin and evil are finally vanquished. The hatred of those who worship whom they choose, according to their own ideas and desires, will continue to foment against those who choose to worship God according to His will and Word. The last chapter in the great conflict between good and evil—the final test—will be *who* to worship. God's dealings with the rebellion of Lucifer, with Cain and his descendants throughout all history, will ultimately be seen as fair, just, and merciful.

Cain's descendants

Cain became the father of a long line of false worshipers who were bold and defiant rebels against the authority of the God of heaven. Because the race lived for centuries, their capability for good or evil was great. The Bible also notes some of the faithful ones who loyally worshiped the Creator. But as time went on, intermingling through marriage and other associations allured God's followers into false worship, and, gradually, the distinction between the two classes of worshipers became blurred.

Cain and his descendants ignored the Sabbath rest commandment, serving the god of this world instead of the Creator God. Murder, polygamy, and depravity of all kinds hardened their hearts, thus spreading sin like a deadly disease. As the Lord looked down, He "saw that the wickedness of man was great in the earth, and that every intent of the thoughts of his heart was only evil continually" (Genesis 6:5). However, in spite of the great wickedness, there were always a faithful few!

God's called-out people

Seth, the son of Adam, became the father of a godly line who "began to call on the name of the LORD" (Genesis 4:26). We cannot even begin to imagine the great mental and physical strength these people inherited from the couple God had made in His own image. They also had the benefit of the presence of Adam and Eve among them for many centuries. They needed no written records, for their memories were far superior to ours. Their mental faculties continued to develop throughout their long lives. For many centuries, seven generations lived on earth at the same time.[5]

Enoch, the seventh from Adam, walked with God for three hundred years and was a man of great piety. This true worshiper spent much time in prayer and was a faithful witness for his God to the people of his generation. After the birth of his first son, Enoch began to understand more deeply God's love for His children and His deep yearning for their welfare. God revealed to Enoch His plan of redemption and the coming of the Messiah. Jude, in the New Testament, portrays Enoch preaching the second coming of Jesus in judgment against sinners (see Jude 14, 15).

As God called Seth, Enoch, and others to represent Him and to appeal to their generations to return to Him and to worship and obey Him, so God called Noah to preach a life-and-death message to his generation, a call to turn from their idolatry and reverence and worship the true God instead. Noah called people to leave their sinful lifestyles and to enter the ark of safety he was building, in order to escape from the Flood that would destroy all life. A merciful God commissioned Noah to preach to these wicked sinners for 120 years. He warned and pleaded with the rebels to repent and turn to God (see Genesis 6). In His omniscience, God knew that none would respond to the call, yet He graciously delayed His judgments for more than a hundred years.

The same call came to Abraham, when he was seventy-five years old. " 'Get out of your country. . . . I will make you a great nation. . . . And in you all the families of the earth shall be blessed' " (Genesis 12:1–3). " 'All the land which you see I give to you and your descendants forever' " (Genesis 13:15). Abraham was not perfect; he made his share of mistakes, but God trusted him. Why? Because everywhere Abraham went he built an altar and called on the name of the Lord—that is, he faithfully worshiped the Lord (see Genesis 12:7, 8).

Abraham and Sarah led others to worship the true God. When they arrived in the "promised land," even though it was filled with idolatry, they built an altar and called their family together for morning and evening sacrifices. What a witness they were to their Canaanite neighbors! Abraham's religion made him a man of courage; as a worshiper of the true God, he became a hero and a deliverer to his neighbors.

During His earthly ministry, Jesus declared to the Jews, " 'Your father Abraham rejoiced to see My day, and he saw it and was glad.' " When they protested, Jesus asserted, " 'Before Abraham was, I AM' " (John 8:56, 58). He who was the Majesty of heaven, the great I AM, came to earth in the form of a tiny baby and took upon Himself human nature. He became one of us, in order to redeem us from our fate. True worship is motivated by the wonder and adoration that humans experience when they sense the greatness and the holiness of their God. Worship is the creature bowing before his Creator, the helpless, penitent sinner falling down at the feet of his Savior and Redeemer! It is the suppliant bowing before a compassionate God, in awe that he is loved and accepted. The human mind cannot grasp or comprehend such amazing and undeserved love. It is the mystery of that divine love that motivates the worshiper to bow humbly and gratefully before his Lord!

Bethel, the "House of God"

Like Adam's sons, Abraham's grandsons, Jacob and Esau, represented two kinds of worshipers. Esau, the hunter, gloried in his freedom in the wild and open fields. There was no room in his life for God. He had no interest in the spiritual responsibilities of the birthright as the firstborn. Jacob's inclinations toward God were strong, and he craved the spiritual birthright that his brother viewed so carelessly. Jacob had flaws that needed to be overcome. Jacob fell for his mother's plan to deceive his father into blessing him with the birthright—with bitter results. From that point on, Jacob's spiritual journey took him through many sad and disappointing experiences, including exile from his home and family. One memorable night on his journey, Jacob had a life-changing dream; he saw angels of God ascending and descending a ladder. When he awoke with the realization that God had talked to him in the dream, he was afraid. " 'Surely the LORD is in this place, and I did not know it. . . . How awesome is this place!' " (Genesis 28:16, 17). There the Lord renewed to Jacob the promise He had given to his father and grandfather, the promise Isaac had repeated to him when he left home: " 'May God Almighty bless you, and make you fruitful and multiply you, that you may be an assembly of peoples; and give you the blessing of Abraham. . . . that you may inherit the land in which you are a stranger' " (verses 3, 4). There on that sacred spot, Jacob set up a pillar, calling it *Bethel*—" 'God's house.' " There he made a vow to faithfully return a tithe to his God (see verse 22).

Is it possible that some of God's children today, like Jacob and Esau, can be exposed to religion, attend church, and go through the motions of worship, without having really met God? They have perhaps been " 'doing church' " from childhood—singing the songs and repeating prayer forms, hearing the sermons and appeals. Some will go their own way and, like Esau, will never find the joy of knowing God personally. Or could it be that some, like Jacob, have never had an encounter with the Lord Jesus Christ? Have never personally glimpsed His glory or seen His love and felt His forgiveness? Like Jacob, they go through the motions, struggle, and fail. Then one day, something happens; the light dawns, perhaps not as startling as Jacob's dream of a ladder to heaven, but a personal message: " 'I am with you' " (verse 15). That simple, short message can be as life changing for us as it was for Jacob! He sensed God's unseen presence. " 'Surely the LORD is in this place, and I did not know it' " (verse 16).

Now, with his focus changed from himself to his God, Jacob, the repentant fugitive, renewed his vows to Jehovah, and there in that sacred spot, which he named Bethel, he worshiped the Lord (see verses 18–22). (Incidentally, this is the first instance in Scripture that speaks of " 'the house of God.' ") Years later, even in his night of wrestling with the Angel, Jacob continued to claim God's promises. In humility, he clung to the angel, insisting, " 'I will not let You go unless You bless me' " (Genesis 32:26). Jacob's sincere repentance, his clinging to the Lord for the assurance of acceptance, his persevering spirit, and his total submission to the Lord's will, were all part of his worship experience. Jacob's struggle with the Lord, refusing to let go unless he received the needed blessing, brought the desired result—he became a new man, now named *Israel,* meaning literally, " 'Prince with God,' " instead of *Jacob,* " 'the Deceiver' " (see verse 28).

The war over worship takes place in every human heart. Who will receive your worship? Who will prevail in your heart? The " 'Jacob-to-Israel' "—" 'Deceiver-to-Prince' " experience is the basis of all true worship and one that every child of God must seek and find personally.

---

1. Karl Tsatalbasidis, "The Emerging Church: More Than Just a Facelift," *Adventists Affirm* 22, no. 2 (Summer 2008): 19.
2. Ellen G. White, *Patriarchs and Prophets* (Mountain View, Calif.: Pacific Press® Publishing Association, 1958), 62.
3. Ibid., 83, 84.
4. Cheryl Wilson-Bridges, *Levite Praise* (Lake Mary, Fla.: Creation House, 2009), 51.
5. White, *Patriarchs and Prophets,* 83.

CHAPTER 2

Worship and the Exodus

The great French sculptor Rodin once created a statue of a famous Frenchman. The lifelike reality of the hands was so amazing that it seemed to dominate the whole statue. Rodin called one of his students and then another and another. Each had the same reaction; the attention of each was focused on the hands. In anger, the sculptor reached for a hammer and smashed the statue's hands! He explained to his stunned students that no single part of a sculpture must dominate the composition. No part is more important than the whole![1]

Although God called Abraham to become the father of a nation that would be known as worshipers of Jehovah, neither Abraham nor any of his descendants were to be the star characters. What God wants us to see in that narrative is His leading, His guidance of a people who would witness to His greatness and power.

Abraham's descendants

The history of Abraham's descendants, including Jacob and his twelve sons and their four mothers, is filled with intrigue, confusion, tragedy, but also with hope! The story of their move to Egypt, where their brother Joseph presided next to a pharaoh, is probably one of the favorites of all the biblical human interest accounts. Between the record of Joseph's death in Genesis 50 and the narrative of the birth of baby Moses in Exodus 2, lie hundreds of years of slavery, untold hardships, tears, and prayers. Those years, difficult as they were, developed the family of Israel from a small tribe to a nation living in one of the most developed and advanced cultures on earth at that time.

Yet that same culture, along with Israel's status as slaves, might have become the source of their demise had not a loving God intervened. While the Egyptians were devout worshipers, their gods were idols of creatures made by the true God—everything from frogs to cows, the sun and moon, even the Nile River! It is hard to imagine the effect that this culture had on the people of Israel in their enslaved circumstances. Some Israelites may have compromised and worshiped Egyptian gods. Others may have not worshiped at all, given their condition. However, there were always those, including the parents of Moses, who remained true to the God of heaven. No doubt, the faithful among them knew of the prophecy given Abraham that they would be afflicted in a strange land for more than four hundred years. Surely they must have clung to the promise that after their affliction they would " 'come out with great possessions' " (Genesis 15:14).

Moses

Jochebed and Amram, true worshipers of God, were among those who believed that the time for their deliverance was at hand. The story is a classic. The infant future deliverer of Israel is found by Pharaoh's daughter on the bank of the Nile; his sister, Miriam, finds a Hebrew nurse (his mother) to care for him. His young life is spent in the courts of royalty!

Some biblical archaeologists believe that 1 Kings 6:1, specifying 480 years from the Exodus to the building of Solomon's temple, dates the birth of Moses to about 1530 B.C. If so, he would have been born during the eighteenth dynasty in Egypt, making it plausible that the princess who found Moses may well have been Hatshepsut, and that the Pharaoh of the Exodus was Thutmoses III.

Though Moses was true to his God, living in the lap of royalty may have tainted him with a bit of arrogance. At least his fellow Israelites seemed to think so, as demonstrated by the incident recorded in Exodus 2 when he killed an Egyptian to begin his role as Israel's deliverer. Later, when Moses tried to intervene between two fighting Hebrews, one immediately asked if he intended to kill him too.

Realizing that his murder of the Egyptian was generally known, Moses fled and found refuge with Jethro, the priest of Midian. There in the wilderness, herding sheep, Moses earned his degree in patience and humility in the "University of Adversity." For forty years, God prepared Moses for the task of delivering and leading His people out of bondage. During those years, Moses, under the inspiration of God, wrote the book of Genesis.[2]

Now God looked down on the afflictions of His chosen people and saw their oppression. The time for their deliverance was ripe, and God had His man!

Moses' call

For Moses, the quiet solitude of the wilderness, his experience as a shepherd, and communion with his God, all contributed to a strong faith and a rich experience with the God of his fathers. He saw the contrast between the false gods of Egypt and the majesty of the God of heaven as revealed in His created works.

One day, watching Jethro's flock, Moses' attention was arrested by a burning bush that didn't burn up! "The Angel of the LORD appeared to him in a flame of fire" (Exodus 3:2). From the bush came a Voice, calling him by name. Because Moses had learned reverence and respect for God, he listened as he approached the burning bush. He was told not to come nearer, but to remove his sandals, for he was standing on holy ground. When Moses heard the voice of God identifying Himself as the God of Abraham, Isaac, and Jacob, he hid his face and was "afraid" (verse 6).

Christians believe that God is present in the appointed place of worship, yet how often we come into His presence as casually as we would enter a place of entertainment! Humility and reverence are to characterize our thoughts and our deportment as we come to worship the Majesty of heaven. The place of worship should be holy ground to us as truly as was the soil surrounding the burning bush. God would like to give each of us a burning-bush encounter as we read His Word and sense His holiness, so that our hearts will burn within us. He desires our worship of Him to be vital, fresh, and life changing!

God could have delivered Israel when Moses was young and self-confident. But instead, He called Moses as a mature, but humble, shepherd, forty years later. Overwhelmed by his assignment to go back to Egypt and deliver God's people, Moses replied, " 'Who am I that I should go . . . and . . . bring the children of Israel out of Egypt?' " In reply, God assured him, " 'I will certainly be with you. And this shall be a sign to you that I have sent you: When you have brought the people out of Egypt, you shall serve [worship] God on this mountain' " (verses 11, 12).

Moses next asked who he should say had sent him (see verse 13). Often we are tempted to ask, "Who am I that I should undertake this task?" When instead, we should ask, as Moses did, "Who shall I tell them sent me?" Our training, our talents, our abilities are not as important as the connection we have with the One who commissions us. God's answer to Moses' question was, " 'I AM WHO I AM.' . . . ' "I AM has sent me to you" ' " (verse 14).

The plagues on Egypt

Though Moses dreaded going back to Egypt, he obediently made the long journey and was met by his brother, Aaron. Together, they called the elders of Israel and shared God's plan to free them from their bondage. "So the people believed . . . then they bowed their heads and worshiped" (Exodus 4:31). The faithful among the enslaved sons of Israel had continued to worship the Creator God to the best of their ability. They were distressed as they saw their children bowing down to false gods. They often cried out to God for deliverance from the corrupting pressures of their idolatrous surroundings.

The Bible says that Moses and Aaron went before Pharaoh and delivered God's command, " ' "Let My people go, that they may hold a feast to Me in the wilderness" ' " (Exodus 5:1). The insulted Pharaoh responded, " 'Who is the LORD, that I should obey His voice to let Israel go? I do not know the LORD, nor will I let Israel go' " (verse 2). It is not stated, but verse 4 suggests that Moses and Aaron asked Pharaoh to allow the Israelites to have their Sabbaths free to worship God. Pharaoh accused them in anger, " 'You make them [the Israelites] rest from their labor!' " (verse 5). The Hebrew word here translated as "rest" is *shabbatt,* a verb form of the word for "Sabbath."

The Pharaoh made the Israelites' labor more difficult; they must also gather the straw they needed. The taskmasters, who were fellow Israelites set over the workers, were beaten if the quotas were not met. It seemed like an impossible dilemma. God assured Moses that He would deliver His people just as He had promised their fathers (see Exodus 6:1–6). He concluded by saying, " 'I will take you as My people, and I will be your God. Then you shall know that I am the LORD your God who brings you out from under the burdens of the Egyptians' " (verse 7).

Again Moses approached Pharaoh with the Lord's request: " ' " 'Let My people go, that they may serve [worship] Me in the wilderness' " ' " (Exodus 7:16). Moses was asking Pharaoh to let the Israelites go out into the wilderness to worship their God, because the sacrifices they would offer involved animals the Egyptians considered sacred and thus would be an offense to them.

God had been patient with Pharaoh. Moses and Aaron had performed miracles to try to convince him, but he only became more rebellious. Now the Lord instructed them to strike the Nile River and turn its water to blood. Not only was the Nile sacred to the Egyptians, it was their source of life. When this failed to move the Egyptian ruler, God brought further plagues on the land. But with each plague, Pharaoh's heart became more hardened. Even the plague of darkness over the whole land did not open his mind to the light Moses was trying to show him. God had announced He would send one last plague that would devastate the proud monarch and his people with the death of the firstborn of everyone in the land, from Pharaoh to the lowliest servant. The plague would include even the firstborn of the animals. Moses was to speak God's words to Pharaoh, " ' " 'Israel is My son, My firstborn. So I say to you, let My son go that he may serve [worship] Me. But if you refuse to let him go, indeed I will kill your son, your firstborn' " ' " (Exodus 4:22, 23).

Tragic as this plague was, it must be seen in the light of the warning God had given the ruler. Many firstborn of Israel, God's firstborn, had already died needlessly through the cruelty of the Egyptians. God had given them ample warning and opportunity.

Now their day of judgment had come.

The Passover

The final blow was about to fall. God's long-suffering patience had been exhausted, and Moses had been forbidden to show his face again in Pharaoh's court. Still, Moses went before the ruler once more with the terrible news that every firstborn in Egypt, except the children of Israel, would be killed at midnight " ' "that you may know that the Lord does make a difference between the Egyptians and Israel" ' " (Exodus 11:7).

God gave Moses specific instructions on how to prepare for the Exodus from Egypt, including the Passover rites the people were to follow. Every household was to kill a lamb, a male without blemish. The blood of the slain lamb was to be sprinkled on the doorpost of every Israelite home as a symbol of the family's faith in God's deliverance. They were to eat the flesh of the roasted lamb, along with unleavened bread and bitter herbs. They were to eat it in haste with their clothes on, belts fastened, sandals on their feet—ready to leave at the appointed moment. The blood on the doorpost was a sign that the members of that household trusted in the merits of God's great sacrifice and that the angel of death would pass over the household, sparing the firstborn of that family.

Though the people of Israel could not see it then, someday God would send His firstborn Son to become their substitute, and ours, shedding His blood, so that the death decree against sin and evil would lose its power. " ' "The blood shall be a sign for you on the houses where you are. And when I see the blood, I will pass over you; and the plague shall not be on you to destroy you when I strike the land of Egypt" ' " (Exodus 12:13).

One of my most vivid childhood memories is this story, which my mother would give as a reading. She would describe a little girl, a firstborn, awaking before midnight and coming to her father, pleading that he show her the blood on the doorpost. He was sure that it was there, but she insisted on seeing it for herself. Finally, when he took her to look, to his horror, the blood was *not* there. He quickly sprinkled the doorpost just before the midnight hour.

There were many homes in Egypt that night where there was no blood on the doorpost. "And there was a great cry in Egypt, for there was not a house where there was not one dead" (verse 30). Pharaoh called for Moses and Aaron, demanding them to go and take their families, their livestock and herds, and leave Egypt. He even asked that they bless him also (see verses 31, 32)!

Moses' instructions on the Passover service were explicit. The Israelites were to tell their children, " ' "This is done because of what the LORD did for me when I came up from Egypt." . . . You shall therefore keep this ordinance in its season from year to year' " (Exodus 13:8, 10).

Throughout their history, the spiritual condition of the people of Israel could be measured by how faithfully they kept the Passover. Often a spiritual revival would be marked with the keeping of the Passover, especially after a period of apostasy. This occurred in Josiah's reign (see 2 Kings 23:21–23), in the days of Hezekiah (see 2 Chronicles 30:1, 5, 23–27), and in the post-captivity period (see Ezra 6:19–23).

While the Passover service commemorated the deliverance of Israel from Egyptian bondage, it was also an important type of the Deliverer to come. When Jesus celebrated the last Passover supper with His disciples, He said, " 'This is My body which is given for you. . . . This cup is the new covenant in My blood, which is shed for you' " (Luke 22:19, 20). He also said something else that is especially important to Christians today: " 'I will not drink of the fruit of the vine until the kingdom of God comes' " (verse 18).

When we celebrate the Lord's Supper, we look back to the Cross and the deliverance it has made possible for us. The Lord's Supper also points us forward to that great marriage supper when we will worship the Lamb and give thanks for His great deliverance and salvation (see Revelation 19:7). We must be part of "the bride" who has made herself ready.

Have you ever noticed how the congregation tends to shrink on Communion Sabbath? Yes, the Bible does say that we should not drink of the cup unworthily (see 1 Corinthians 11:27), but all of us are worthy only because of Christ. Yet God has given us this sacred ordinance as a part of our worship of Him. It commemorates the death and sacrifice of our wonderful Savior whom we worship. How can we walk away from it? It is to be a little foretaste of that great supper we will eat with Him in the kingdom to come. Dare we absent ourselves from an ordinance that encapsulates our salvation experience and points forward to the time when we will stand around His throne and sing that great song of victory in the grandest and most sublime worship service ever?

Mount Sinai

About two months out of Egypt, the children of Israel came to Mount Sinai out in the desert wilderness. They had already experienced God's care for them in giving them water from a rock, providing food in the form of manna, and protecting them from the assault of the Amalekite enemy. Now, God called Moses up to the top of Mount Sinai, reminding him of His covenant promise to Israel (see Exodus 19:3–7). He told Moses that He was about to give the people the conditions of the covenant. The instructions were explicit: the people were to gather to hear God speak, but they must not come too near the mount, lest His glory destroy them. They were to prepare their hearts—and even their clothes and physical bodies—for this unique experience of God's presence in their midst.

On the third day, "Moses brought the people out of the camp to meet with God, and they stood at the foot of the mountain" (Exodus 19:17). The mountain seemed to be on fire; it smoked, and the earth shook (see verse 18). Again, the people were warned not to come too close lest they perish in the presence of God's glory.

The first four of the Ten Commandments that God spoke there on Mount Sinai had to do with how they should worship God. (We will look at these commandments in chapter 3.)

Worship of the golden calf

Meanwhile, during those forty days while Moses was on the mountain with God, the people became restless, especially the mixed multitude who were accustomed to visible idols. Now this God of Israel who had appeared in such glory was nowhere to be seen! They wanted a god they could see! They came to Aaron, who was in charge during Moses' absence. " 'Come, make us gods that shall go before us; for as for this Moses . . . we do not know what has become of him' " (Exodus 32:1). The story is familiar. They took off their gold earrings and brought them to Aaron. According to the story he would later tell Moses, he just threw all this gold in the fire, and out came a golden calf! He built an altar for it, and the people proclaimed, " 'This is your god, O Israel, that brought you out of the land of Egypt' " (verse 4).

Meanwhile, up on Mount Sinai, God said to Moses, " 'Go, get down! For your people whom you brought out of the land of Egypt have corrupted themselves' " (verse 7). As Moses and Joshua headed toward the camp, Joshua exclaimed to Moses, " 'There is a noise of war in the camp' " (verse 17). Moses replied in essence that it was not the sound of combat, but of singing and revelry (see verse 18). When Moses saw what was taking place around the golden calf, his anger was so great that he threw down the tablets of stone and broke them at the foot of the mountain, symbolizing the fact that the people had broken their covenant with God—the covenant they had made so recently.

Aaron did not have the courage to stand against the mixed crowd. He could have prevented the apostasy, but his compliant spirit emboldened the mixed crowd in this act of treason.[3] "Now when Moses saw that the people were out of control—for Aaron had let them get out of control . . . —then Moses stood in the gate of the camp, and said, 'Whoever is for the LORD, come to me!' " (verse 25, 26, NASB).

Moses dealt quickly and severely with those who attempted to lead Israel into heathen idolatry. God had revealed Himself to Israel as a God of glory and majesty only a few weeks before this. He had given two commandments of the ten that identified Himself as the one and only true God and prohibited worshiping idols of any kind. The Creator God knows that human beings become like what they worship. By beholding we become changed, transformed into the image of who or what we worship (see 2 Corinthians 3:18). God invites us to fix our eyes on His character and goodness in order that we might be changed into His image—not that of some dumb beast or even of another sinful human being.

God is a God of mercy and compassion, and Moses knew Him well enough to go to Him and plead for his wayward people: " 'Yet now, if You will forgive their sin—but if not . . . blot me out of Your book' " (Exodus 32:32). Moses, as a type of Christ, interceded for his people, willing to suffer in the place of his people in order to save them! He was assured that " 'My Angel shall go before you,' " but the penalty for the people's sin must run its course (verses 34, 35).

God is no less holy today than He was then! His glory and majesty are no less brilliant and impressive, even though our earthbound eyes cannot behold Him! His justice and hatred of evil and idolatry have not changed. The adapting of heathen rituals and worldly practices to our worship of the Creator God are no less offensive to Him now than on the day that Aaron made the golden calf!

His mercy and compassion for the repentant are no less gracious and powerful now than they were then. That's why He sent His own beloved Son to demonstrate His love and mercy toward us! That demonstration should motivate and inspire us to give Him the best we have in worship.

We still worship the same God as did Israel of old. He longs to have us come to Him. The conditions of His covenant are the same for us as they were for His people then—obey His revealed will; keep the commandments; show love, reverence, and respect to this wonderful God.

The more we behold His beautiful character, the more He will transform us into His own image. Therefore, as we become partakers of His divine nature, our worship will become less earthly and more in harmony with the heavenly worship of His adoring angels. Every time we worship our majestic God—wholeheartedly and in reverence and awe of His glory—we are practicing for that greatest of all worship services above!

---

1. Robert Spangler, *First Things First* (Washington, D.C.: Review and Herald®, 1977), 90.
2. See White, *Patriarchs and Prophets,* 251.
3. See ibid., 323.

CHAPTER 3

The Sabbath: A Memorial in Time

The pyramids of Egypt, monuments in the sands of time, are actually memorials to dead pharaohs. Grave robbers and the ravages of time have taken their toll, but these huge marvels of an early culture still amaze us. Long before Egypt came on the scene of action, the God of heaven had created a grand monument in time, a monument that could be experienced by anyone, anywhere! His monument is a day—the climax of the weekly cycle that would memorialize His great work of creation!

False worship vs. true worship

In the previous chapter we noted that the enemy of God had hoped to destroy the identity of the descendants of Abraham by enslaving them and leading them into idolatry. If he could not totally destroy them through slavery, he could at least distort their worship of the Creator by leading them to mingle heathen customs and traditions in their service to God, as illustrated in the incident involving the golden calf.

Satan hoped to so pervert their worship that they would lose the sense of God's holiness and majesty and eventually worship him instead of the Creator—as did their heathen neighbors. He would try to accomplish this by getting them to worship senseless man-made objects or even things made by the hand of the Creator. Either would have a degrading effect on the worshipers, leading to licentiousness and pandering to the evil passions of the human heart. For human beings can never rise higher than that which they worship. This has been demonstrated repeatedly in various heathen worship systems.

God's rules for worship

That is why on Mount Sinai, the God of the universe proclaimed to this new nation of His, " 'I am the LORD your God. . . . You shall have no other gods before Me. You shall not make for yourself a carved image—any likeness of anything that is in heaven above, or that is in the earth beneath . . . you shall not bow down to them nor serve [worship] them' " (Exodus 20:2–5). Even God's name, Yahweh, is holy, and He instructed them not to use it carelessly or in vain (see verse 7).

God's claim to worship and honor is based on the fact that He created the human family and all things in the universe, and only He has the power to change perverted human nature. The worship of false gods, on the other hand, always tends to degrade rather than uplift the human character, because of the very nature of these false gods.

A monument for worship

God did not only give instructions on what *not* to do regarding worship. After three commands prefaced by "You shall not," He gave a positive command: " 'Remember the Sabbath day, to keep it holy. Six days you shall labor and do all your work, but the seventh day is the Sabbath of the LORD your God. In it you shall do no work. . . . For in six days the LORD made the heavens and the earth . . . and rested the seventh day. Therefore the LORD blessed the Sabbath day and hallowed it' " (verses 8–11).

The Sabbath of the Lord teaches us:

1. *Whom we should worship*—the Creator God who made us.
2. *When we should worship*—the seventh-day Sabbath, which He instituted at the end of Creation week as a monument in time, a day set apart in which to worship the Creator.
3. *How we should worship*—a whole twenty-four-hour day set aside for the worship and honor of God, a day for spiritual rest.
4. *Why we should worship*—because the Creator God gave us a Sabbath rest to keep us in touch with our Divine Maker.

This monument was to constantly remind the human family that we originated from the hand of the Creator. Yet through all time, the enemy has attempted to destroy God's holy day or to obliterate its significance. If all else failed, he would try to replace it with a false replica—another day!

A sign of God's covenant

Therefore, God explicitly emphasized that this day was to be a sign of His perpetual covenant with His people. " 'The seventh day is the Sabbath of the LORD your God [literally, "the LORD's Sabbath"]' " (verse 10). The Sabbath, God says, " ' "Is a sign between Me and you . . . that you may know that I am the LORD who sanctifies you. . . . Therefore the children of Israel shall keep the Sabbath . . . throughout their generations as a *perpetual covenant*" ' " (Exodus 31:13, 16; emphasis supplied).

The Sabbath was the sign of the covenant relationship between God and His people. They were set apart from all other people of the earth because God had called them out to be a holy people, sanctified by His grace and power. Every Sabbath day would be a special day of worship, a witness to the world around them of the blessings of being part of His covenant people. The weekly Sabbath was also to teach His people, then and now, about the true God, about how to worship Him, and about the blessings and benefits of worshiping Him!

The enemy hates the Sabbath because of its power for good! He wanted Israel then, and he wants us now, to forget that the Sabbath is a sign that " ' "in six days the LORD made the heavens and the earth" ' " (verse 17).

Geologists dig up so-called evidence that the earth is millions of years old. Evolutionists continue to insist that the origin of life came through a strange accidental mix of molecules in some prehistoric slime. However, the Sabbath day, as found in Genesis 2, stands as an irrefutable monument to God's creative power. " ' "It is a sign between Me and the children of Israel forever" ' " (verse 17). "So long as the heavens and the earth endure, the Sabbath will continue as a sign of the Creator's power."[1] "To all who receive the Sabbath as a sign of Christ's creative and redeeming power, *it will be a delight.*"[2]

A sign of deliverance

Shortly before his death, Moses rehearsed the Ten Commandments as part of his farewell address to the people. He reminded Israel that it was God who had brought them out of Egypt " ' "by a mighty hand and by an outstretched arm; therefore the LORD your God commanded you to keep the Sabbath day" ' " (Deuteronomy 5:15). The Sabbath was not only to be a memorial of God's creative power, but a commemoration of His deliverance of the Israelites from Egyptian bondage. The Sabbath rest is a reminder of our deliverance, too, from the power of sin through Christ and is more than enough reason to celebrate our salvation by keeping holy His sacred day.

Jesus Himself offers His rest as a remedy for our human ills. " 'Come to Me, all you who labor and are heavy laden, and I will give you rest. Take My yoke upon you and learn from Me, for I am gentle and lowly in heart, and you will find rest for your souls' " (Matthew 11:28, 29). Every seventh-day Sabbath that rolls around in the weekly cycle is to bring spiritual rest, as well as physical relief, to the bodies, minds, and souls of those who have found rest in Jesus.

The apostle Paul is emphatic on this point in his letter to the Hebrews, reminding them that God rested from His work of Creation and wants us to enter into spiritual rest by ceasing our labors as He did. Israel of old, under Moses, Joshua, and others, often failed to learn that lesson. So Paul reminds us that God is still waiting for His people today to enter into the spiritual rest of trusting Him instead of their own works, symbolized by the rest of the seventh-day Sabbath (Hebrews 4:9). "Today if you will hear His voice: 'Do not harden your hearts' " (Psalm 95:7, 8). So today there still remains a rest for us, a true spiritual rest of not just the body, but of the heart and soul, resting by faith in what He has promised to do for us through His grace.

Examples in Israel's history

A careful examination of Israel's history verifies that the people's standing with God was often measured by their relationship to the Sabbath day. The prophets often linked their apostasy to their carelessness in Sabbath keeping.

The prophet Isaiah ministered in the days when Assyria was a threat to Judah and the northern kingdom was already in its declining years. In the first chapter of his book, Isaiah warned Judah that sacrifices and observing feasts, the Sabbaths, even their prayers, were not acceptable as long as the people had blood on their hands (see Isaiah 1:5–15). Later, he pronounced a blessing on those who refrain from defiling the Sabbath (see Isaiah 56:2, 6–8). In chapter 58, Isaiah made an appeal for true Sabbath keeping, enumerating the blessings that would follow. The prophet clearly predicted the restoration of the Sabbath day by a people who would be called the " 'Repairer of the Breach.' " As a result, God would cause them to " 'ride on the high hills of the earth, and feed . . . [them] with the heritage of Jacob' " (verses 12, 14).

The prophet Jeremiah ministered during the reign of the last few kings of Judah; his career spanned the transition into the Babylonian captivity. He described in cryptic language the problem of his people: " 'My people have been lost sheep. Their shepherds have led them astray. . . . *They have forgotten their resting place*' " (Jeremiah 50:6; emphasis supplied). The Hebrew word translated "resting place" is often used in a pastoral setting, as in a safe place for flocks to lie down to rest. The Sabbath is a safe place for God's people to rest. When they wander away from their safe resting place, they expose themselves to dangers capable of destroying them!

Ezekiel, a contemporary of Daniel and a captive in Babylon, lived by the river Chebar. In chapter 20 of his book, Ezekiel reviews Israel's history. He quotes God as saying, " ' " 'I gave them My statutes and showed them My judgments, "which, if a man does, he shall live by them." Moreover I also gave them My Sabbaths, to be a sign between them and Me. . . .Yet . . . they greatly *defiled My Sabbaths. . . . They . . . profaned My Sabbaths, and their eyes were fixed on their fathers'* idols' " ' " (Ezekiel 20:11–13, 24; emphasis supplied).

Both Ezra and Nehemiah, in the post-Exile reforms, stressed the keeping of the law. Nehemiah's Sabbath reforms are recorded in chapter 13 of his book. The experiences of Ezra and Nehemiah, as well as those of others, make it evident that the breakdown of Sabbath keeping among God's people was the pivotal point on their road to apostasy. Reformation often began by a revival of true Sabbath observance. How do we know when we need revival and reformation? Our enjoyment of the Sabbath rest (or lack of it), like a thermometer for a person who is ill, may well indicate whether or not there is a problem!

The gift that meets human needs

Rest is a basic human need. The Sabbath rest is a gift that ministers to our needs at every level—whether for physical rest to refresh a tired body or emotional rest to calm a troubled heart or spiritual rest to renew a lagging or dying spirit. Let's take a closer look at this gift.

Psychologist Abraham Maslow was the designer of a model now known as "Maslow's Hierarchy of Needs." His thesis was that the most basic human needs—

such as air, water, and food—are the most powerful motivators. Emotional and psychological needs come in for attention after our most basic needs are met. For example, you don't talk to a dying man in the desert about his need for acceptance or for love, because nothing else really matters if his need for water is not met immediately! However, once you minister to his physical needs, you will no doubt find other areas of need in his life as well.

The God who made us knows our needs at every level of our being, and He has given us the Sabbath rest to provide for those needs and to meet us at every level of our being. Yes, the Sabbath is designed to be a relief from physical labor, thus we are to rest from our routine work on the Sabbath day. But the Sabbath is more than that. It also provides us with emotional rest from the ordinary problems of life; we set them aside while we celebrate God's holy day.

The Sabbath gives us a special day set aside from the ordinary, the mundane, and the urgent. It reminds us of God's willingness to forgive us and cleanse us from sin. The Sabbath tells us that we are the children of God, that we are important to Him, and that He loves us! It speaks to us of our value, our worth, for He made us upright, in His own image, and He wants to restore us to that image. The Sabbath brings balance and perspective into our lives. It gives us an opportunity to rest our minds from the routine as an antidote to boredom and to lift them to that which is beautiful in God's great handiwork of nature and in His Word. Above all, the Sabbath rest allows us to enjoy and relish the experience of worshiping our God, our wonderful Creator and Redeemer. We have twenty-four hours set aside just for being with Him and enjoying what He has given us to be a blessing!

The Sabbath reminds us that we have aesthetic needs—those for beauty and the finer things of life. The Sabbath is a day to admire and enjoy God's great handiwork, which is still beautiful in spite of the ravages that sin has caused. His purpose is to restore His image in us and others, which can best be accomplished as we permit Him entrance into our lives and allow Him to show us the true meaning of His holy Sabbath day, the promise of His power for our restoration. God's Sabbath keeping people must be experts in sharing the healing message of the Sabbath.

Finally, the Sabbath points forward to a great future: eternity with God. Therefore, the Sabbath is the promise of hope, giving meaning and purpose to life. The Sabbath invites us to enjoy God as we draw into a closer relationship with Him in the Sabbath hours. "To comprehend and enjoy God is the highest exercise of the powers of man."[3]

A call to worship the Lord

"Oh come, let us worship and bow down; let us kneel before the LORD our Maker" (Psalm 95:6). This beautiful psalm, a call to worship the Lord, also contains a plea for sinner-saints to stop hardening their hearts as Israel did, resulting in their wandering in the wilderness for forty long years (see Hebrews 4:8–11). Why would the psalmist interrupt this lovely praise psalm to make this urgent appeal? Because he knew Israel's history so well and how often they had failed to meet God's purpose for them.

Paul quotes from Psalm 95 in his appeal to the Hebrew Christians to whom he was writing. He pleads with them to enter God's rest and not to refuse God's appeal as did Israel of old when they hardened their hearts. The Sabbath rest is a symbol that we have stopped trying to earn our salvation by "doing" good works. Rather, we are to accept the rest of salvation, symbolized by resting from our daily work on the Sabbath.

Paul addresses his own Jewish people, wanting them to see that Christ is greater than Moses and that it is the Holy Spirit speaking in Psalm 95 to them and to us: " 'Today, if you will hear His voice, do not harden your hearts as in the rebellion, in the day of trial in the wilderness, where your fathers tested Me, tried Me, and saw My works forty years' " (Hebrews 3:7–9).

Paul is challenging his hearers to understand that because of Israel's unbelief and disobedience, they wandered in the wilderness for forty years when they could have entered the Promised Land—the rest God had promised. Some of Paul's statements, taken out of context have been used to negate the keeping of the Sabbath day. For example, Hebrews 4:8 refers to Joshua speaking of "another day," which some have said means that the seventh-day Sabbath has been changed to Sunday, the first day of the week. But Paul is referring to Joshua 22:4 where Joshua says, " 'The LORD your God has given *rest* to your brethren' " (emphasis supplied). Unbelief kept Israel from entering both the spiritual rest of trusting obedience and the rest of entering the Promised Land. Later, when they acted in faith and obeyed God's commands, they entered the rest that came with possessing the land.

Paul's message, though sometimes misunderstood, is a powerful appeal to all of God's children. God desires obedience based on faith and love. His purpose is that we *enjoy His Sabbath rest as a symbol* of *our salvation, rather than as a way of earning salvation!* Resting in His salvation is a foretaste and promise of our inheriting the rest of the heavenly Canaan when He comes to set up His kingdom.

God's invitation to us today

God has given us the Sabbath rest to be a blessing in our own lives, physically, emotionally, and spiritually. It is a day in which to honor Him as our Creator and as our Redeemer. It is a day set apart from the six working days in which we labor and work to meet our own needs. The Sabbath is a day set aside for us to spend time with our Creator God. The Sabbath has been given to us as a day of worship in which we are to honor God with our adoration, our praise, our gifts, our devotion, and our worship.

It is a time for looking forward to the final Sabbath rest when we will see our Savior and Lord face-to-face and fall at His feet and worship Him saying,

> "You are worthy, O Lord
> To receive glory and honor and power;
> For You created all things,
> And by Your will they exist and were created" (Revelation 4:11).

The Sabbath is a time for us to prepare for that great day when we will join the saved of all ages in singing the victory song of the redeemed: "And every creature which is in heaven and on the earth and under the earth and such as are in the sea, and all that are in them, I heard saying: 'Blessing and honor and glory and power be to Him who sits on the throne, and to the Lamb, forever and ever!' " (Revelation 5:13).

By God's grace we must be there!

---

1. Ellen G. White, *The Desire of Ages* (Mountain View, Calif.: Pacific Press®, 1940), 283.
2. Ibid., 289; emphasis supplied.
3. Ellen G. White, *Our High Calling* (Washington, D.C.: Review and Herald®, 1961), 61.

CHAPTER 4

God's Blueprint for Worship

The more we know about God, His holiness, His character, and His self-revelation, the better we will understand how to worship Him. Worship must flow from a heart that is filled with wonder and adoration for the God we love.[1] In this chapter we will look at God's great model for worship as found in the wilderness sanctuary, with its blueprint given to Moses by God Himself.

Make Me a sanctuary

" 'Let them make Me a sanctuary, that I may dwell among them' " (Exodus 25:8). How would this command have sounded to you, had you been out there in that desolate wilderness? How impossible it must have seemed to the children of Israel! No lumber yards, no hardware stores, no construction crews! Yet, God had a plan for a place where He could meet with His people. Better yet, He desired to *dwell* with them. He had already provided the materials. Now *they* were to bring what they had collected from their Egyptian masters and neighbors (see Exodus 12:35, 36). " 'Speak to the children of Israel, that they bring Me an offering. From everyone who gives it willingly with his heart you shall take My offering' " (Exodus 25:2).

God had carefully planned the blueprint for a portable sanctuary and its furnishings as well as its assembly and disassembly for carrying it from place to place in their wilderness wanderings. Detailed instructions were given for every aspect of the sanctuary and its services. The people's response to God's request for offerings would determine the success of the project.

" ' "Whoever is of a *willing heart,* let him bring . . . an offering" ' " (Exodus 35:5; emphasis supplied). Notice that the willing heart comes before the offering. Both are important, but in the right order. God's people gave with generous hearts, bringing all kinds of materials for the work (see verses 22–35). Eventually, the craftsmen came to Moses and said that the people were bringing too much (see Exodus 36:3–7). What a great problem to face!

The word *worship* as used in Scripture, comes from a Hebrew word that means to prostrate oneself before an important personage or royalty, to give homage, to bow down, or to give obeisance and reverence.

While bowing our knees before our Maker is important, we also worship and show homage to Him by giving of our material substance as we honor Him by supporting His work. The people of Israel gave of their best! They gave willingly for the Lord's house. Every gift we bring to our God—whether tithes, offerings, talents, or time—is to be brought *as an act of worship.* He is honored and delights to bless us by accepting them.

Israel's wilderness temple was the center and focus of their worship experience. Every rite, feature, and furnishing within the ancient sanctuary given to Moses by God, illustrated important principles of worship. Even now, we may learn much about how God would have us worship Him as we consider Israel's model sanctuary.

Turn your back on false worship

The door (literally a curtain) to the court faced east. Thus, worshipers coming into the court would always have their backs to the rising sun. Many of the ancient heathen religions worshiped the sun. God warned His people, by this simple arrangement, against the satanic counterfeit worship so prevalent in their day. Centuries later, the prophet Ezekiel saw worshipers in the temple facing the east and worshiping the sun. He warned them of God's severe judgment against their sin (see Ezekiel 8:15–18). If we think that item of sanctuary practice has no relevance to us today, we need only observe some of the current trends in worship. For example, a book published in 1990 exposed New Age attempts to infiltrate fundamentalist Christian churches with their Eastern cult teachings and practices.[2]

On a more positive note, the gate of the court was the entrance into the house of worship. David suggests how we are to approach God's house: "Enter into His gates with thanksgiving, and into His courts with praise. Be thankful to Him, and bless His name. For the LORD is good; His mercy is everlasting" (Psalm 100:4, 5).

New Testament priests

"Everything connected with the apparel and deportment of the priests was to be such as to impress the beholder with a sense of the holiness of God, and the sacredness of His worship, and the purity required of those who came into His presence."[3] Peter reminds us that in the New Testament era, we Christians are "a royal priesthood, a holy nation, His own special people" (1 Peter 2:9).

Thus, as we come to worship God in His house, it would be helpful for us to remind ourselves that we are part of God's priesthood. If Christ has placed on us His spotless robe of righteousness, we should—out of gratitude for His gift—reflect and exemplify His character in our behavior, and even in our dress and appearance, especially when we come into the very presence of the King of the universe to worship Him. Jesus told a parable about a man who came into a wedding hall as a guest, but when the host saw that he did not have on the proper wedding attire, he was thrown out (see Matthew 22:11–13).

The sacrifice God desires—prerequisite to worship

The altar of burnt offerings, located in the outer court near the gate, was the first station of service in the sanctuary. Every morning and evening, a year-old lamb was offered on the altar of burnt offerings by the priests. This unblemished lamb symbolized Christ (see 1 Peter 1:19).

The daily sacrifices on the altar of burnt offering were to remind God's people that worship is a daily matter. Morning and evening we need to confess our sins and receive His forgiveness. In addition to the daily sacrifices offered by the priests, a sinner might bring his offering of a lamb. He was required to cut the lamb's throat. The priest would then take the blood and sprinkle it around the altar of burnt offering.

To illustrate the significance of this ritual, let's fast-forward to the story of Israel's beloved King David. The prophet Nathan had come to the king to tell him a parable about a rich man who took the life of the only lamb a poor man owned. David was angry and pronounced a death sentence on the unjust rich man. Then, Nathan declared the shocking sentence: " 'You are the man!' " (2 Samuel 12:7).

Picture the scene: The king comes to the sanctuary with his lamb, cuts its throat, and watches as the blood drips from the innocent animal! (Remember,

David had been a shepherd.) The guilty king stands there filled with self-condemnation, remorse, and humiliation. No wonder he cries out, "Have mercy upon me, O God, according to Your lovingkindness; according to the multitude of Your tender mercies, blot out my transgressions" (Psalm 51:1). He admits that he deserves God's judgments (see verses 3–5). He prays for restoration (see verse 12). Then, David, looking at the poor innocent lamb that has been sacrificed for his terrible sin, utters a surprising statement: "You [God] do not desire sacrifice . . . You do not delight in burnt offering" (verse 16). Why did David say that? Because he understood that the sacrifices God really desires are "the sacrifices of . . . a broken spirit, a broken and a contrite heart—these, O God, You will not despise" (verse 17).

What does this story have to do with worship? Quoting Dr. Bridges again, "True worship is initiated and empowered by the Godhead, which was symbolized by the animal sacrifice that foreshadowed Christ's death."[4] The spirit of penitence and sorrow for sin are the only ways into God's presence, the only paths to authentic worship of a Holy God. Before entering the sanctuary, atonement for sin must be made. Before we come to worship God, we must do what David did—we must come to God with a broken spirit, a heart that realizes its sinfulness and calls on God for forgiveness and cleansing.

Paul suggests that we are to "present . . . [our] bodies a living sacrifice, holy, acceptable to God, which is . . . [our] reasonable service" (Romans 12:1). The word *service* here implies an act of religious service or worship. *What God is really looking for is the whole person—body, spirit, and heart.*

The laver—a place for cleansing

The laver, a place for washing, was in close proximity to the altar of burnt offering. Here the priests would wash their hands and feet before entering the Holy Place or before ministering at the altar of burnt offering. It was a place of cleansing prior to appearing before God, teaching that all sin and defilement must be put away before coming into God's presence.

David begged the Almighty for a clean heart (see Psalm 51:10). Likewise, when we appear before a Holy God, we, too, must pray for cleansing and put away all sin as we come to worship Him. Paul suggests that God wants to sanctify and cleanse His people "with the washing of water by the word" (Ephesians 5:26). As we are immersed in His Word and as we spend time with our God in meditation and prayer, we will be cleansed and purified by His grace. With this cleansing, we are ready to worship our God!

Worship and the bread of the presence

The table of shewbread was located in the Holy Place and always had twelve loaves of bread on it. The Hebrew word translated as *shewbread* means "bread of the presence." The bread represented Christ, who is in the presence of God for us. " 'For the bread of God is He who comes down from heaven and gives life to the world.' . . . And Jesus said to them, 'I am the bread of life. He who comes to Me shall never hunger, and he who believes in Me shall never thirst' " (John 6:33, 35). The people's response to Jesus was, " 'Lord, give us this bread always' " (verse 34).

When leading in worship, pastors have the privilege and responsibility of feeding their congregations with the bread of the presence. We do not receive this bread by hearing mere philosophy, men's opinions, entertaining stories, or humanistic theories. Only the solid spiritual bread, Jesus Christ and His Word, will nourish our souls and produce spiritual growth.

Worship and the golden candlestick

The beautifully wrought candlestick, formed from one piece of gold, was opposite the bread of the presence. It may have weighed as much as two hundred pounds. The translators of the New King James Bible estimate the value of a talent of gold at over a million dollars, using the 1983 standard.

The purpose of the seven-branched candlestick was to give light. It was lit every day, constantly supplied with pure olive oil. Jesus declared that He is the Light of the world (see John 8:12). He promised the Holy Spirit (symbolized by the oil) to His followers to guide them and prepare them to be His witnesses (see John 16:7–15).

The oil of the Holy Spirit was the source of the fire in the hearts of the apostles. It lit a fire in the hearts and lives of both Jews and Gentiles, who spread Christianity in those early days with supernatural power to the whole then-known world!

Today, we, too, need to receive that same cleansing by fire—the Holy Spirit power—in order for our worship of a Holy God to be acceptable. As we come to worship Him, the Holy Spirit convicts us of sin, encourages us with forgiveness and acceptance, and assures us of His love. Then with hearts cleansed and humbled, we give Him permission to fill us with His Spirit, so that we may reflect His light to a world darkened by sin.

The altar of incense and our Great High Priest

The altar of burnt offering was made of bronze, but the altar of incense was covered with gold. The high priest was to offer incense upon this altar every morning and every evening, as a perpetual offering before the Lord. Though the altar of incense was actually located in the Holy Place, it was " 'before the mercy seat' " (Exodus 30:6). Thus, in a sense, it belonged to the Most Holy Place. The cloud of incense ascended before the mercy seat, above the ark of the covenant—the holy chest containing the tablets of stone on which God Himself had written His holy law with His own finger. Those commands had been broken, and now atonement had been made. The incense ascending before that sacred chest was the symbol of the intercession of the Great High Priest to come.

The sanctuary worshipers were to engage in earnest prayer, searching of hearts, and confession of sin. No offering they might bring, no confession they might make, could absolve them from their transgressions. Only the death of a substitute, prefiguring the ultimate Sacrifice, could pay their debt. Even more important, they needed an intercessor, someone worthy who could defend them.

"Seeing then that we have a great High Priest who has passed through the heavens, Jesus the Son of God, let us hold fast our confession. . . . Let us therefore come boldly to the throne of grace, that we may obtain mercy and find grace to help in time of need" (Hebrews 4:14, 16). "We have such a High Priest, who is seated at the right hand of the throne of the Majesty in the heavens, a Minister of the sanctuary and of the true tabernacle which the Lord erected, and not man" (Hebrews 8:1, 2). "Therefore He is also able to save to the uttermost those who come to God through Him, since He always lives to make intercession for them" (Hebrews 7:25).

Ellen White suggested that even the best we have to offer God in acts of worship—prayers, praise, penitent confession of sin, even obedience—because they come through the corrupt channels of our sinful human nature, are unacceptable to God unless they are offered up by our Intercessor, who applies His blood with the incense of His own precious righteousness. The fragrance of that incense ascends like a cloud around the mercy seat.[5]

Talk about good news! It doesn't get any better than that. When we worship and give our best, it still isn't good enough; however, our Great High Priest in the heavenly sanctuary, Jesus Christ, constantly makes intercession in our behalf. He takes our feeble worship and offers it up before the Father with the fragrant incense of His own righteousness! That wonderful truth has the power to change our hearts, our attitudes, our behavior, and our worship!

The Shekinah glory

We learned in chapter 1 that the Shekinah glory resided outside the gate of the Garden of Eden, where Adam and Eve and their descendants worshiped for many years. That same Shekinah glory resided above the ark of the covenant containing the Ten Commandments and the mercy seat (see Exodus 25:16–22). God's presence made the sanctuary so holy that only the priests and Levites were allowed in its sacred precincts. Yet, the Shekinah glory was only a dim reflection of the glorious temple in heaven.

When we invoke God's presence in our worship services today, we are inviting the same Holy God whom Israel worshiped to meet with us! He is no less holy now than He was then. How important that as we approach Him in worship, we do so with awe, respect, and honor!

The Biltmore estate in Asheville, North Carolina, is perhaps the most beautiful and well-preserved structure of its kind in the United States. Often, as people view some of the large, impressive rooms of this mansion, a hush comes over the group, and voices drop to a whisper in awe of what they are seeing. Perhaps we need to ask ourselves, Has worship become so commonplace to us that we forget that the house of worship is the place where God comes to meet with us? Have we lost our sense of awe at the greatness and majesty of our God? He wants to meet with us, as He did with Israel of old, but we must come in reverence and respect for His holy presence.

The more we contemplate His greatness and majesty, as well as His condescending love and mercy, the deeper will be our wonder, admiration, and humility as we come into His sacred presence.

---

1. A. W. Tozer, *Worship and Entertainment* (Camp Hill, Pa.: Wing Spread Publishers, 1997), 18, 23.
2. Will Baron, *Deceived by the New Age* (Nampa, Idaho: Pacific Press®, 1990), chapters 5, 8, 9.
3. White, *Patriarchs and Prophets,* 351.
4. Wilson-Bridges, *Levite Praise,* 53.
5. White, *Selected Messages,* 1:344.

CHAPTER 5

The Foundation of Worship: Faith or Presumption?

Worship is not simply a specific physical act, such as kneeling in prayer. Rather, it is the condition of a heart that loves and adores God, a heart that has been humbled before a great and mighty Creator. It is a heart that has been broken at Calvary, devoted to the death of self, and committed to the lordship of Jesus Christ. Such a heart is not looking for self-fulfillment but for the glory of its Maker and how He desires to be approached. In the Christian world today, many believe they have the right to choose the form or style of worship that seems appropriate for them.[1]

In this chapter we will look at several Bible stories that illustrate two classes of worshipers—those who presumed to think they could worship in their own way, and those who were intent on worshiping God in faith and obedience. The lessons are pregnant with meaning for every Christian who wants his or her worship to honor the God of heaven!

According to Hebrews 11:1–3, faith is based on God's Word and therefore is a reliable and safe foundation on which to build our religious beliefs. Presumption, on the other hand, is an opinion or a belief based on a conjecture or a false premise that we assume to be factual.

Nadab and Abihu: Leviticus 10:1-11

The first example of presumption we will look at is one of the saddest in Scripture. Nadab and Abihu, Aaron's sons and Moses' nephews, had been chosen as priests. They had been privileged to be on Mount Sinai when God ratified His covenant with Israel (see Exodus 24:1). They had been instructed regarding their work in the sanctuary.

Aaron and his sons had been consecrated to the priesthood by anointing with oil and sacrifices of blood. Aaron had blessed the people of Israel. The glory of the Lord had appeared, as fire consumed the sacrifice. Awed by this token of God's glory, they praised the Lord and bowed before His majestic presence. High privilege carries with it high responsibility! These men had been carefully instructed. They knew the rules, but they presumed to think that high privilege allowed them certain liberties. The record implies that they had imbibed too much intoxicating drink, confusing their ability to make wise choices (see Leviticus 10:8–11). Rather than using fire from the altar of burnt offerings for their censers, as instructed, they presumed that ordinary fire might work just as well. The scripture says simply that "fire went out from the LORD and devoured them, and they died before the LORD" (verse 2). What a tragedy! Was God being too severe? What if He had let this incident pass? God is too holy and just to allow human beings to ignore His specific instructions. His people must learn that presumption is a terrible sin, especially to be avoided by those who lead in worship!

Some would argue that God was too severe, that He should have given these men another chance. Yet God had specified to Moses and the leaders that everything connected with His service was to be done according to His blueprint. Nothing was to be done in a haphazard or careless manner. Notice God's words spoken through Moses following this incident, " ' "By those who come near Me I must be regarded as holy; and before all the people I must be glorified" ' " (verse 3).

God Himself had kindled the fire for the altar of burnt offering; there was to be no substitute. Fire represents the Holy Spirit. The enemy delights in replacing God's Spirit in human hearts with his own rebellious spirit. It is dangerous to think that we can create our own power for worship when God has given specific instructions that only worship consistent with, and inspired by, the Holy Spirit can be accepted. God wanted to teach Israel that He is to be approached in reverence and awe. He required the people to make a difference between the common and the holy.

Yet in our day, there is a popular religious movement that accepts anything that pleases carnal hearts as appropriate for worship. Such an idea is based on the assumption that there is no difference between the secular and the sacred, the profane and the holy.[2]

Our wonderful and Holy God deserves our honor, our reverence, and our devotion in order to worship Him who is worthy of our very best!

The sin of complaining: Numbers 11

The new nation of Israel had been camped at Mount Sinai for about a year. They had witnessed many miracles, including water from a rock and daily manna for food. Now, as they resumed their journey through the barren wilderness, they began to complain about the food. They were tired of manna and wanted flesh to eat. The complaining and discontent was contagious. What had probably started with the mixed crowd, made up of Israelites who had some Egyptian blood, now spread throughout the camp. Moses, though a very humble man, was overwhelmed with the complaining. " 'I am not able to bear all these people alone, . . . the burden is too heavy for me' " (Numbers 11:14). Instead of trusting God, Moses panicked. God's answer to him was, " 'Has the LORD's arm been shortened?' " (verse 23). Now God would give the people what they asked for, by a disciplinarian miracle! He provided more quail than they could possibly eat, accompanied by a plague—perhaps bird flu? (See verse 33.)

What can we learn from this story? Although complaining and whining are common human weaknesses, they must not, and cannot, dwell in the heart that truly worships and adores a holy and omniscient God. To question God's leading to the point of rebellion is the fruit of presuming to think that we know better than God what is good for us, that our way is better than what God has planned for us.

Jealousy in the family: Numbers 12

The next crisis to afflict Moses was a family problem. Jealousy is a subtle evil that appears innocent enough in its embryo stage but can quickly grow and become infectious. Moses' sister, Miriam, who had watched over her baby brother as he lay in a basket in the Nile River, now began whispering her discontent to brother Aaron. In their conversation they said, " 'Has the LORD indeed spoken only through Moses? Has He not spoken through us also?' " (Numbers 12:2). The siblings also disliked that Moses married a Cushite. How often our criticism of others is based on our own natural prejudices and dislikes—even jealousy and envy, as in the case of Miriam. We place more confidence in our biased opinions than in facts, leading us to presumptuous attitudes, if not sin.

Again, the Lord took rather drastic measures to let Miriam and Aaron know that indeed He had chosen their humble brother, Moses, to lead His people. Because Miriam had *presumed* to judge Moses, she became leprous. Only when Moses interceded in her behalf did God remove the plague.

To find fault with spiritual leaders is easy; after all, they are human! Moses was *human,* and though humble, he also made mistakes! This story is recorded to help us understand that God does not tolerate criticism of those He has appointed to lead His people. There is no room in any human heart for true worship while cherishing feelings of jealousy, envy, and criticism. The grace of God is strong enough to deliver us from these very human tendencies!

Insubordination and conspiracy: Numbers 16

Rebellion breeds insubordination. God's judgments seemed to restrain the spirit of rebellion for a time, but eventually it cropped up again, this time in a deeply laid conspiracy led by Korah, a Levite, and a cousin of Moses.

"The children of Korah were assigned to the ministry of music and song at the sanctuary services."[3] Evidently Korah's abilities caused him to aspire to the priesthood (see Numbers 16:10). The men whom Korah gathered around him were well-known leaders. Forgetting that the Angel of the covenant was their real Leader and rebelling at the thought of wandering in the wilderness for forty years, they pursued their conspiracy with what appeared to be religious zeal. The conspirators spread their evil accusations against Moses and Aaron among the congregation. Korah would be a much better leader, they claimed. He would encourage the people, all of whom, he claimed, were holy, instead of pointing out their faults.

By the time Moses became aware of Korah's deeply laid plot, it had become full blown. He fell on his face before the Lord in a beautiful example of true humility, begging for direction from his God. Moses' faith in God's guidance was deep and based on the many wonderful evidences and miracles of His leading. Moses' response to Korah was quick. " 'Tomorrow morning,' " he said, " 'the LORD will show who is His and who is holy' " (verse 5). God gave the rebels time to reconsider their conspiracy. Moses instructed them to come with their censers and to put fire and incense in them. Confident that the Lord would make clear who was the true leader of His people, Moses called for Korah's fellow conspirators, Dathan and Abiram, but they refused to come. The Hebrew word for "come up" (verse 12) is a legal term, meaning "to appear in court." Moses was giving them an opportunity to submit their case to arbitration.

On the following day, "every man took his censer . . . and stood at the door of the tabernacle . . . with Moses and Aaron" (verse 18). Korah called for the congregation to come to the tabernacle to witness his victory in taking over the leadership of Israel. "Then the glory of the LORD appeared to all the congregation" (verse 19). The Lord instructed Moses to warn the people to stay away from the tents of the conspirators. Furthermore, Moses declared, " 'If these men die naturally like all men . . . then the LORD has not sent me' " (verse 29). We cringe at the tragic scenario that followed—the earth split apart and swallowed up all of the conspirators and their company.

Was God being too harsh with them? Or by intervening was He protecting His people from a massive disaster? It is hard to imagine the chaos that would have resulted had these angry rebels been allowed to carry out their wicked plot. Korah and his company had cherished envy and jealousy against Moses until it had become full-blown rebellion. They had resisted the Holy Spirit, and they had rejected evidence that God was leading Moses, until they actually deceived themselves into thinking that they were doing God's work. They had rejected light so long that even the most striking manifestation of God's authority they credited to another power. They presumed they were doing God's work, when in fact they had become agents of evil.[4]

The path of presumption in any form is a dangerous road to travel. Our only safety in the Christian life is to have a deep and abiding faith in God's instructions as revealed in His Word. Our worship experience must come from a humble heart, totally submitted to the Lord Jesus Christ.

Hannah, a woman of faith: 1 Samuel 1

Leaving the children of Israel in the wilderness, we now move forward to the time of the judges. This was a difficult period in Israel's history. Many of the judges were a great disappointment to God. Even the priesthood had become corrupt. God was looking for a good leader. Hannah, a godly woman who grieved because she could not bear children, came to the temple with her husband. The record states that "she was in bitterness of soul . . . and wept in anguish" when Eli, the high priest, accused her of being drunk (1 Samuel 1:10). It was obvious to all the people that Eli's sons were wicked, immoral men, not fit for the office they held. As much as Hannah wanted a son, this perceptive woman also saw the spiritual conditions in Israel and prayed that God would give her a son who might fill the need. This is evidenced by the fact that she dedicated her son to be under a lifelong Nazirite vow (see verse 11).

She explained herself to Eli and he told her to " 'Go in peace' " (verse 17). The record says that Hannah ate, and "her face was no longer sad" (verse 18). Early the next morning before returning to their home, Hannah and Elkanah "rose . . . and *worshiped before the Lord*" (verse 19; emphasis supplied).

Samuel: 1 Samuel 3; 4

Samuel was the answer to his mother's prayer and a nation's need! Imagine the emotional conflict that must have rent Hannah's heart as the time approached for her to fulfill her pledge to the Lord. She knew the kind of environment to which Samuel would be exposed. However, she had made a vow to God, and she must commit her son into His hands. What faith! God rewarded both her prayers and her faith by calling Samuel to the prophetic office. God spoke to him while he was still a young lad. Eli's counsel to Samuel was wise. When God called Samuel, he was to say, " ' "Speak, LORD, for Your servant hears" ' " (1 Samuel 3:9). This should be the prayer of every true worshiper. We need God's counsel and direction, and He is pleased when we listen to Him speak to us. Samuel grew and matured, and the Lord was with him. He revealed Himself to Samuel in Shiloh where the sanctuary was located, and all Israel came to understand that Samuel was a prophet (see verses 19–21).

God had indicated to Samuel that Eli's house must be judged. The nation was about to face a test. The Philistines attacked the Israelites and defeated them. The elders of Israel had felt that their only protection was to take the ark of the covenant from Shiloh to lead the army (see 1 Samuel 4:3–5). In this, they were following the custom of the heathen nations to have their gods lead their armies. These leaders *presumed* to use the ark as a god. When the Philistines realized what was happening, they said, " 'God has come into the camp! . . . Woe to us!' " (verse 7).

When Israel recognized God's instructions, He blessed them. When they saw the sacred ark as a mere "magic idol," it became little more than a common box so far as God was concerned.[5]

Is it possible even in this age that professed Christians may seek to form their ideas of God and how to worship Him according to a kind of pagan Christianity with its secularized customs and philosophies?

Ichabod—the glory has departed: 1 Samuel 4-7

The battle ended in tragedy and a great slaughter, but most tragic of all, the sacred ark was captured. Eli, the high priest, was ninety-eight years old. When he heard the news about the ark, he fell over and died (see verses 17, 18). His daughter-in-law went into labor upon hearing the news and gave birth to a son (see verses 19, 20). In her dying moments, she named him Ichabod, meaning " 'the glory has departed from Israel' " (verse 21). Indeed, because of Israel's sins, the glory of God's presence had departed.

Eventually, the ark was returned, but not before the men of Beth Shemesh were struck down because they looked into it. This tragedy prompted Samuel to call his people to reform. " 'If you return to the LORD with all your hearts, then put away the foreign gods . . . and prepare your hearts for the LORD, and serve [worship] Him only' " (1 Samuel 7:3). The people responded, and there was a revival that day. Samuel set up a stone as a memorial and called it Ebenezer, meaning " 'thus far the LORD has helped us' " (verse 12).

Does our generation need revival? Has the glory—the fervor of the pioneers of this movement—departed from us? Do we need to repent, put away our favorite gods, and return to God with all our hearts? Yes, we, too, need an Ebenezer experience for " 'thus far the LORD has helped us!' "

Obedience better than sacrifice: 1 Samuel 8-10; 13; 15

All too often human nature wants to play god! We think we know what we need better than God does. Samuel had made his sons judges over Israel, but, like Eli, he had not been a good disciplinarian. So now the elders of Israel came to Samuel, requesting that since his sons were not following in his footsteps the people needed a king to lead them, such as all the nations around them had. The Lord told Samuel that the complaint was not directed at him, yet Samuel was devastated. He prayed to the Lord, and the Lord replied, " 'They have not rejected you, but they have rejected Me' " (1 Samuel 8:7).

Israel was a theocracy; God was their king. But they wanted to be like the nations around them. Sound familiar? Many Christians today seek to imitate the practices of worldlings, even in worship, with the objective of winning friends to Christ. Instead, all too often it wins Christians to the world!

A king for Israel came by God's permission, not His will. Saul, tall and handsome, appeared like a man born to command—just the man that fit Israel's ideal for a king to rule over them (see 1 Samuel 9:2). Samuel revealed to Saul that he would be king over Israel. The Spirit of God came upon him. The Lord gave him a new heart, and Saul worshiped with the prophets (see 1 Samuel 10:10–12).

Then Samuel called the people together at Mizpah and anointed Saul publicly as the new king over Israel. The prophet carefully explained the "behavior of royalty, and wrote it in a book" (1 Samuel 10:25). Samuel instructed Israel and the new king that the nation's success depended upon their faithfulness and obedience to God. However, the young king quickly forgot the instructions of the prophet. He "felt compelled," that is, he *presumed* to offer a sacrifice, which only a priest could perform. "What he lacked in real piety he would try to make up by his zeal in the forms of religion."[6]

Samuel must have been heavy hearted as he reminded Saul that his kingdom would not continue (see 1 Samuel 13:13, 14). Yet God gave the king another opportunity to demonstrate loyalty to His commands. Samuel had instructed Saul that in going to battle against the Amalekites, Israel was to " ' "utterly destroy all that they have" ' " (1 Samuel 15:3). Saul presumed to have a better way; he would bring back the booty and use it for sacrifice. Samuel was grieved and cried out to the Lord all night. Saul's greeting to Samuel the next morning was an outright lie: " 'I have performed the commandment of the LORD' " (verse 13). Samuel, perhaps with tears in his voice, confronted the presumptuous king. " 'What is more pleasing to the LORD: your burnt offerings and sacrifices or your obedience to His voice? Listen! Obedience is better than sacrifice, and submission is better than offering the fat of rams. Rebellion is as sinful as witchcraft, and stubbornness as bad as worshiping idols' " (verses 22, 23, NLT). God could not have been more offended had Saul offered his sacrifice to a heathen idol. When Saul later consulted the witch at Endor, it was the consummation of his rebellion against God.

God does not delight in sacrifices and burnt offerings as such. What He really wishes is a penitent and obedient heart. Religious services and worship are an insult to God when given by those who persist in the willful violation of even one of His commands.[7] The same God who prompted Samuel's words to Saul of old, wants His children in this age to remember that He will not be bought off by unholy sacrifices, no matter how good they may appear to human eyes! We dare not presume to set our own standards of how we are to come to Him in worship. The sacrifices we bring to Him must be with sorrow for sin and a willingness to obey regardless of the cost!

Such worship will ascend to our God as sweet incense, for He longs to bless those who worship Him with surrendered hearts.

---

1. See Tozer, *Worship and Entertainment,* 18.

2. See Tsatalbasidis, "The Emerging Church," 23, 24.

3. Francis D. Nichol, ed., *The Seventh-day Adventist Bible Commentary* (Washington, D.C.: Review and Herald®, 1978), vol. 1, 875.

4. See White, *Patriarchs and Prophets,* 405.

5. Ibid., 584.

6. Ibid., 622.

7. Ibid., 634.

CHAPTER 6

David and Solomon: Architects of Worship

Ralph Waldo Emerson wrote, "Prayer is the contemplation of the facts of life from the highest point of view. It is the soliloquy of a beholding and jubilant soul."[1] If you have stood at the edge of the Grand Canyon and tried to grasp its immensity, feeling the smallness of your own life by comparison, you have experienced a bit of the feeling that prompted Emerson's jubilant soul!

Worship is a matter of perspective, a perspective of one's own smallness in view of the Grand Canyon. More pertinent to our topic of worship, it is the perspective of the wise men who, having traveled many miles to find the Messiah, realize that this tiny babe at the end of their journey is the fulfillment of the prophecies they have been studying for years. They are awed by the incongruity of the circumstances in which they find Him, but they know instinctively, for their jubilant souls assure them, that this indeed is the long looked-for Messiah!

David and Solomon were also jubilant souls who, in spite of human weaknesses, made significant contributions to our understanding of how God should be worshiped. Both were used by God to shape and enhance Israel's worship. In this chapter we will look at some of their accomplishments.

David, a heart for God

God chose Saul to be the first king of Israel, according to the model the people wanted. Both Saul and David manifested human weaknesses; both were sinners. From a mere human viewpoint, David's transgressions seem graver than Saul's, overall. Yet there was this difference: when Saul was reproved, he pouted and rebelled against the Lord. When David was reproved, he repented and cried out to God for a clean heart. When sinful human beings refuse to repent and reject God's forgiveness, they eventually cut themselves off from His grace and mercy. This is what Saul did.

David's connection with God began as he watched his flocks on the Judean hillsides. He often raised his voice in praise and worship with the songs of his own composition, inspired by the Holy Spirit. No wonder David was called the "sweet singer of Israel." Whenever David was faced with danger—whether by a lion, an angry Saul, or a Goliath—he had a courageous heart. Most important, David had a heart for a God. When Saul presumed to act the part of a priest by offering sacrifices instead of waiting for Samuel, the prophet informed him, " 'Your kingdom shall not continue. The LORD has sought for Himself a man after His own heart' " (1 Samuel 13:14). That man was David.

When David faced Goliath, he made it clear that the Lord was going to deliver the giant into his hand, " 'that all the earth may know that *there is a God in Israel*' " (1 Samuel 17:46; emphasis supplied). When Saul was in trouble, he took things into his own hands. When David was in trouble, he called on God.

David was a flawed human being with struggles and weaknesses; however, he had a heart for God; his heart was tender and open to his Maker, willing to listen to God. Even when the guilty David was confronted with the prophet's parable of a rich man stealing the only lamb of the poor man, he humbly recognized that his own declaration of a fourfold penalty was just and fair in light of his sin (see 2 Samuel 12:1–14).

A heart for God, then, is one that admits its sinfulness, but cries to God for forgiveness and renewal. It is a heart that is willing to accept God's discipline and move on to begin again. It is a heart that puts God's honor above one's own wishes and desires. Such a heart worships God from the depths of its love for Him, even in spite of human failures. The prayer of David should be the prayer of every true worshiper: "Search me, O God, and know my heart; test me and know my anxious thoughts. Point out anything in me that offends you, and lead me along the path of everlasting life" (Psalm 139:23, 24, NLT).

David and the ark of the covenant

David had a holy zeal for his God, the kind of zeal that should motivate every worshiping child of God. Once David became established on the throne of Israel, he turned his attention to a cherished objective. For many years, the ark had remained at Kirjath Jearim. Now that his kingdom was well established, David made impressive preparations to transfer the ark to his new capital. David's zeal was contagious! Thirty thousand leading men in Israel helped to make the event an imposing occasion. Suddenly, amid the celebration and music, there was a terrible tragedy. Uzzah touched the ark to steady it, and he died instantly! David had failed to study the instruction book! This holy symbol of God's presence must never ride on a cart, but it was always to be carried by the Kohathites, who were to lift it by staves placed in rings on the side of the ark (see Numbers 4:15).

David's motives were right, but his methods were faulty; just as today many may have sincere motives in worship but use faulty methods that are not acceptable to God. Following Uzzah's death, David turned to the divine instructions to be sure that every detail was carried out according to God's plan. He carefully planned for the sacred ark to be handled with appropriate reverence. This ark contained the two tablets of stone on which were written God's Ten Commandments for humanity, written with God's own finger. In Israel's sanctuary, this ark was surrounded with the Shekinah glory—God's own holy presence. Humans, in their spiritual blindness, forgot that "the LORD reigns; let the peoples tremble! . . . The LORD is great in Zion. . . . He is holy" (Psalm 99:1–3).

After praying and studying God's instructions, David planned another occasion for the transfer of the ark to his new capital. This time he would be sure that every detail was according to God's plan. This time, the king laid aside his royal robes and wore a common robe and a tunic similar to that worn by the priests, thus showing his identity with his subjects. David's dancing before the Lord was "in reverent joy before God."[2]

The musical instruments for this sacred occasion were limited to those used in holy worship, avoiding percussion instruments commonly used in secular celebrations (see 1 Chronicles 13:6–8; 15:16–29). The bitter comments made by Michal, David's jealous wife, have been used to imply that he behaved in an inappropriate way. Unfortunately, her bitter accusations are also sometimes used as a platform for inappropriate styles of worship and for including entertainment in worship.

As a sacred symbol of Israel's invisible King, the ark was holy, and those who ascended the holy hill of Jerusalem that day, including David, needed to be pure and holy as well (see Psalm 24:1–6). Imagine the triumphal procession. A choir bursts forth in song, as the ark makes it way to Jerusalem:

> Lift up your heads, O you gates!
> And be lifted up, you everlasting doors!
> And the King of glory shall come in.

The antiphonal choir responds, "Who is this King of glory?" Then the answer returns, "The LORD strong and mighty, the LORD mighty in battle" (Psalm 24:7, 8).

The service that marked the transfer of the ark to Jerusalem was a lesson to the people of Israel about God's sanctuary and its sacred services. David made music and song a part of religious worship, giving to Israel and all succeeding generations a heritage of hallowed music that reminded them of God's leading in their past history and that praised and honored Him for His majesty, His holiness, His greatness, and the assurance of His leading in the future.

The hymn of worship that David wrote for this special occasion is recorded in 1 Chronicles 16:8–36. Read the complete hymn. Notice how often David uses active verbs to describe acts of worship:

- "Give thanks to the LORD!" (verse 8). *A grateful heart, a life lived in gratitude to God, is an act of true worship.*
- "Make known His deeds among the peoples!" (verse 8). *Preaching the great deeds of the past stimulates worshipful attitudes.*
- "Glory in His holy name" (verse 10). *Worship brings honor and glory to His holy name—speak it reverently.*
- "Seek His face" (verse 11). *Come into His house to seek His holy presence, and He will be found.*
- "Sing to the LORD" (verse 23). *Sing songs of praise and adoration to Him who is worthy of praise.*
- "Remember His marvelous works." "Proclaim the good news of His salvation" (verses 12, 23). *The mind filled with His goodness will want to proclaim His greatness.*
- "Remember His covenant forever" (verse 15). *Covenant keepers will show their love to God by faithful obedience.*
- "Give to the LORD the glory due His name" (verse 29). *Those who carry*

His name will seek to honor Him in everything.

- "Bring an offering" (verse 29). *Giving tithes and offerings is an act of worship as much as is prayer and praise.*
- "Come before Him" (verse 29). *Come humbly, come bowing, come confidently, and worship God in awe.*
- "Worship the LORD in the beauty of holiness!" (verse 29). *Holiness is beautiful. God is pleased when we offer our best in worship.*

Worship is action! God wants our worship to be genuine, joyous, and wholehearted. David's song suggests many ways by which we may worship Him. Worship is something we give to God. He is the object of our worship. Worship is not about us—what we like, what makes us feel good! God is the only One worthy of our worship!

A house for God

David had built a palace for himself. He had brought the ark to his capital. Now he determined to build a house for God. He shared his dream with the prophet Nathan who gave him his blessing. Then God communicated to Nathan that it was not in His plan for David to build a house for Him. David's hands had been stained with blood, and as dedicated as he might be, the honor of building a house for God must be left to his son Solomon.

Perhaps one of the greatest evidences of David's heart for God is embedded in this story. His submission to God's will, his resignation of his cherished plan, is a lesson for every Christian whose hopes or plans have been dashed! To yield to another what we hoped to do for God, to resign our dreams and goals for someone else to fulfill, though painful at times, may be God's finishing touch on a life preparing for worship in heaven.

Although David would not be allowed to build a house for God, the Lord promised that He would build David "a house" (1 Chronicles 17:10). This promise was to be fulfilled in the coming of the long-looked for Messiah. On the Day of Pentecost, Peter quoted Psalms 16:8–11; 68:18; 110:1 as proof that Jesus Christ was indeed the promised Son of David, Israel's Messiah (see Acts 2:22–36). The highest honor that ever came to David was the house God built for him as the progenitor of the Messiah—Jesus Christ, Son of David!

David's preparation for the temple

The intriguing story of how David purchased Ornan's threshing floor, the very spot on which the temple would eventually be built, is recorded in 1 Chronicles 21:18–30. As king, David might have demanded that Ornan give him the property. Instead, the king insisted on paying him the full price, another evidence of David's generous nature.

First Chronicles 22 records in detail David's plans and efforts to provide everything needed for building the temple once Solomon came to the throne. According to David's instructions, all temple musicians were ministers, that is, Levites, who were also trained musicians, directing and performing the music of worship (see 1 Chronicles 15:16–22; 16:4–6).

David's prayer at Solomon's coronation

David had made it official that his son Solomon would be his successor and would build the temple " 'not for man but for the LORD God' " (1 Chronicles 29:1). He charged his people, " 'Be careful to seek out all the commandments of the LORD your God, that you may possess this good land, and leave it as an inheritance for your children' " (1 Chronicles 28:8). He then charged Solomon, " 'Know the God of your father, and serve Him with a loyal heart and with a willing mind. . . . If you seek Him, He will be found by you' " (verse 9)

At Solomon's coronation, David offered a beautiful prayer of thanksgiving. " 'For all things come from You, and of Your own we have given You' " (1 Chronicles 29:14). David prayed for his people that they would give willingly; he prayed that his son Solomon would be faithful in keeping God's commandments and that he would build the temple for which David had made provision (see verses 16–19). This was King David's last public appearance of his forty-year reign. His contributions to Israel were numerous. His legacy to the Israelites, as well as to Christians today, lives on in his prayers and songs of worship, for he served the King of the universe!

"You are my King, O God" (Psalm 44:4).
"Your throne, O God, is forever and ever" (Psalm 45:6).
"The LORD Most High . . . is a great King over all the earth" (Psalm 47:2).
"Mount Zion [is] . . . the city of the great King [God]" (Psalm 48:2).

Solomon builds the temple: 2 Chronicles 2; 3

The very first public act of Solomon's reign was to call the leaders and the congregation together at Gibeon, which was still the location of the official tabernacle of meeting. There, Solomon offered sacrifices and humbly prayed for wisdom and counsel to judge his people (see 2 Chronicles 1:1–3)

Chapters 2 and 3 of 2 Chronicles describe Solomon's selection of helpers, building materials, and the careful planning for every detail of this temple for God. Ellen White describes Solomon's temple as being "of surpassing beauty and unrivaled splendor. . . . Garnished with precious stones . . . lined with carved cedar and burnished gold."[3]

Here on the very spot Solomon built the temple, Abraham had offered Isaac, and God had renewed with him the covenant, including the Messianic promise.[4] Here, now stood this beautiful edifice Solomon had built for his God. "So all the work that Solomon had done for the house of the LORD was finished" (2 Chronicles 5:1).

Solomon chose the Feast of Tabernacles as the time for the dedicatory service. This feast was a happy occasion, coming as it did at the end of the harvest season. People would come from all over Israel to witness the dedication of Solomon's temple.

Solomon's prayer of dedication: 2 Chronicles 6

As he addressed the congregation, Solomon stood on a bronze platform built for the occasion in the temple court. He reminded the people that God Himself had chosen Jerusalem as the place where His name would be glorified in the temple, which David had wanted to build. Now God's plan had been satisfied; Solomon had accomplished what his father had begun to the honor of God's name in this temple of worship.

Then Solomon solemnly knelt before the congregation and prayed one of the most impressive and touching prayers recorded in all of Scripture: " 'LORD God of Israel, there is no God in heaven or on earth like You, who keep Your covenant and mercy with Your servants' " (2 Chronicles 6:14). He reminded God of His promise to David that his posterity, if obedient, would continue to rule over Israel (see verse 16). He humbly acknowledged that no temple built with human hands could contain God. " 'Behold, heaven and the heaven of heavens cannot contain You. How much less this temple which I have built!' " (verse 18). Yet the king boldly implored

God to hear his prayer for the people. He asked God to turn His eyes toward this temple day and night, to hear the supplications of His people when they prayed toward this place (see verses 20, 21).

Solomon knows his people, so in his prayer he lists the troubles they may face because of their sins against their neighbors and against God: defeat before an enemy, drought, famine, pestilence, blight, mildew, locusts and grasshoppers, and besiegement by an enemy (see 2 Chronicles 6:24–28). Then he pleads with God that " 'when they pray toward this place [the temple] and confess Your name, and turn from their sin because You afflict them, then hear in heaven, and forgive the sin of Your servants, Your people Israel, that You man teach them the good way in which they should walk' " (verses 26, 27).

Solomon's prayer is the architectural foundation for true worship. The temple, the place of worship, is the place where sinful human beings come to receive what only God can give—forgiveness for sin, acceptance back into God's favor, and spiritual support for obedience. To those who know what they should do but have failed, to those who have wandered into a far country of rebellion, to those caught up in sudden temptation, to a people who have been careless in living the new life—to all who feel disconnected from God for any reason—the invitation is, *return*! Solomon's prayer assures us that God will forgive, He will reconnect us, He will heal us and restore us! Furthermore, He promises that if we are willing, He will cause us to walk in His ways (see verse 31).

Solomon's prayer goes beyond God's own people. If there are foreigners (those who don't belong to God's people or who are strangers to spiritual things), God's grace is available to these individuals if they come and pray in His temple (see verse 32). Why is the temple open to them? Because God wants all the people of the earth to know His name and fear Him (see verse 33). God's house of worship, then, is a place where all people may come for forgiveness, for renewal, for comfort in sorrow, for help with daily burdens—to connect, or reconnect, with their God. Solomon prays for God's eyes to be open and His ears attentive to the prayers made in the temple. His prayer ends with an appeal to God to " 'remember the mercies of Your servant David' " (verse 42).

At the end of Solomon's prayer, "fire came down from heaven . . . and the glory of the LORD filled the temple" (2 Chronicles 7:1). The children of Israel were so awed by this wonderful manifestation that "they bowed their faces to the ground on the pavement, and worshiped and praised the LORD, saying: 'For He is good, for His mercy endures forever' " (verse 3). That glorious moment would be etched in their memories for the rest of their lives!

What would happen today if God's house, like Solomon's temple, were to be filled with awe and reverence, with the Holy Spirit hovering over the worship service? What would it be like to see people coming to the church to meet God because they have seen what He does for their friends who worship there? What would happen if when people came, they saw their friends filled with the Holy Spirit, praising God, living the new life?

What would happen today in our churches if more prayers were patterned after Solomon's prayer? What victories might be won in lives? What new commitments might be made? What connections restored? What revivals might begin in the church? What would happen if people came because they saw a church on fire with a holy zeal, and they wanted to experience God in the same way? True worship will provide God's people and a world in need of His grace with these victories, these commitments, these revivals!

What a challenge to God's people today to be faithful in our worship of Him! God wants us to avoid aping the cheap and entertaining worship so prevalent in our society. He wants our best in worship, as He alone deserves to be worshiped!

"Although God dwells not in temples made with hands, yet He honors with His presence the assemblies of His people. He has promised that when they come together to seek Him, to acknowledge their sins, and to pray for one another, He will meet with them by His Spirit. . . . Unless they worship Him in spirit and truth and in the beauty of holiness, their coming together will be of no avail."[5]

---

1. Ralph Waldo Emerson, *Self-Reliance and Other Essays* (Nashville: American Renaissance, 1841), 42.
2. White, *Patriarchs and Prophets,* 706, 707.
3. Ellen G. White, *Prophets and Kings* (Mountain View, Calif.: Pacific Press®, 1943), 36.
4. Ibid., 37.
5. Ibid., 50.

7

CHAPTER

The Psalms: Treasures for Worship

Sir Isaac Newton once had someone make a miniature replica of our solar system. A scientist entered his study and exclaimed, "What an exquisite thing this is! Who made it?"

Newton knew the scientist was an unbeliever, so he said, "Nobody!"

The questioner replied, "You must think me a fool; somebody had to have made it, and he was a genius."

Whereupon Newton put his hand on the scientist's shoulder and said, "If you insist that this mere toy had a maker, how can you profess to believe that the great original came about without a designer or a maker?"[1]

The creation psalms tell us that the Living God, the Creator of heaven and earth, alone is worthy of our worship! He created all things, while gods of wood or stone are mere figments of human imagination. Many in our world no longer believe in a Creator God, choosing rather to attribute the marvels of human life and the wonders of the world around us to mere chance or implausible evolutionary theories that attribute matter to an accidental meeting of molecules, millions of years in the past. Whether the false god is an idol of clay or a so-called scientific theory, it is still a poor substitute for the true God, who created this planet and its inhabitants.

Since the inception of sin, there have always been those who have developed alternate explanations for the origin of human life in an effort to deny the existence of the Creator God of the universe. Darwin, who at one time planned to be a preacher, was motivated by a desire to deny the existence of God, for he was appalled, understandably so, at the idea that a good God would torture bad people in hell for all eternity.

The creation psalms emphasize that God in His greatness as Creator of heaven and earth deserves the worship of His creatures. "What is man that You are mindful of him? . . . For you have made him a little lower than the angels" (Psalm 8:4, 5). The response God's creatures owe Him is expressed with vigor.

"Oh come, let us worship and *bow down*; let us *kneel* before the *Lord our Maker*. For He is our God" (Psalm 95:6, 7; emphasis supplied). "Know that the Lord, He is God; *it is He who has made us,* and not we ourselves" (Psalm 100:3; emphasis supplied). "Let Israel *rejoice in their Maker*" (Psalm 149:2; emphasis supplied).

One of the oldest of the psalms, written by Moses, declares that the everlasting God, *Creator of the universe,* existed before the creation of our world. Therefore, He deserves our worship. "Lord, You have been our dwelling place in all generations. Before the mountains were brought forth, or ever You had formed the earth and the world, even from everlasting to everlasting, You are God" (Psalm 90:1, 2), and Psalm 92 is titled "A Song for the Sabbath Day." It begins with an invitation to sing praises to God, Most High. "You, Lord, have made me glad through your work. . . . How great are Your works!" (verses 4, 5).

Sacrifices of righteousness

Worship, then, is the right response to this great God who has created the universe and everything in it. And when we come to God in worship, we are to bring to Him our offerings of prayer, praise, petition, and gifts. According to Paul, God asks us to give ourselves (our bodies) as a "living and holy sacrifice. . . . This is truly the way to worship Him" (Romans 12:1, NLT).

Scripture frequently refers to the "sacrifices of righteousness." The first mention of this phrase pictures one of the tribes of Israel offering righteous sacrifices (see Deuteronomy 33:19). The term is found several times in the psalms. Psalm 4:5 reads simply, "Offer the sacrifices of righteousness." *The Seventh-day Adventist Bible Commentary* says of this text that these sacrifices are "sacrifices prompted by right motives out of a sincere heart."[2] In the NLT, Psalm 4:5 reads, "Offer sacrifices *in the right spirit*" (emphasis supplied).

Psalm 51 states that the sacrifice of righteousness is "a broken and a contrite heart," as we noted in an earlier chapter (see verse 17, 19). Perhaps the clearest implication of the meaning of the sacrifice of righteousness is found in the Messianic prophecy of Psalm 40: "You take no delight in sacrifices or offerings" (verse 6, NLT). God was not pleased with those who went through the form of the sacrificial ritual, expecting the ritual itself to be meritorious, without having the heart of the suppliant. The psalmist continues with words spoken by the Messiah: "I said, 'Look, I have come. As is written about me in the Scriptures: I take joy in doing your will, my God, for your instructions are written on my heart' " (verses 7, 8, NLT).

Paul reminds us in Hebrews 10:1–5, that the Old Testament sacrifices were insufficient to deal adequately with sin, because the blood of bulls and goats could not in reality remove sin; these sacrifices were merely symbolic. He then quotes Psalm 40:6–8, commenting that "we have been sanctified through the offering of the body of Jesus Christ once for all" (Hebrews 10:10).

To those who desire a genuine-heart religion, the new covenant promise is, " 'I will put My laws into their hearts, and in their minds I will write them . . . their sins and their lawless deeds I will remember no more' " (verses 16, 17). Clearly then, the real righteous sacrifice was the dying body of Jesus Christ hanging on a cruel cross! That sacrifice was for every human being who ever lived or who ever will live and applies to all who accept it. "Therefore, brethren, having boldness to enter the Holiest by the blood of Jesus, by a new and living way . . . let us draw near with a true heart in full assurance of faith" (verses 19–22).

What a glorious promise to every true believer in Jesus Christ! We come to worship God, bringing our sacrifices of repentance, dedication, gratitude, and thanksgiving, and our vows of faithfulness, loyalty for service, for obedience to His commands—all from a heart of love and devotion to Him. Christ is pleased with our response, and the incense of His perfect righteousness ascends to the Father with our less-than-perfect worship sacrifices! Yes, we give Him our best in worship, tainted as it is coming from our human weakness, but our gracious Savior takes our services of worship, adds His own cleansing blood to our sacrifices, and offers them up with the precious incense of His pure righteousness.[3]

So as we come to worship Him—with song and praise, on bended knee in supplication, sharing our testimonies, giving our tangible offerings, allowing the spoken Word to penetrate our hearts and minds—we may picture Jesus offering up our acts of worship with the sweet incense of His pure, holy life so that they ascend in a cloud around the mercy seat. Only His intercession in our behalf can make our worship acceptable! For Christ has entered "into heaven itself, now to appear in the presence of God for us" (Hebrews 9:24). "Therefore He is also able to save to the uttermost those who come to God through Him, since He always lives to make intercession for them" (Hebrews 7:25). Praise God! Worship coming from redeemed sinners is acceptable to God because of the intercession of our Lord Jesus Christ! Hallelujah!

Worship is remembering

The word *remember* is found in more than a hundred references in the Old Testament. God says to "remember His covenant" (1 Chronicles 16:15), " 'remember the Sabbath day' " (Exodus 20:8), "remember His marvelous works" (1 Chronicles 16:12), " 'remember the former things' " (Isaiah 46:9), " 'remember and do all My commandments' " (Numbers 15:40), " 'remember your Creator' " (Ecclesiastes 12:6), etc.

In an article titled "Things We Don't Talk About No More," Russell Baker writes, "We consume our history so fast to get on to the next tidbit that there is no time to digest it, and so we become a people without memory."[4] God says, " 'Remember the former things' " (Isaiah 46:9). A well-known quote from the pen of Ellen G. White states, "We have nothing to fear for the future, except as we shall forget the way the Lord has led us, and His teaching in our past history."[5]

Before Moses died, he wrote the book of Deuteronomy, a series of admonitions to his people, to remind them of God's leading during their wilderness wandering. His fatherly heart ached for them. Several times in the first few chapters, he pleads with them, " 'Take heed . . . lest you forget' " (Deuteronomy 4:9); " 'Beware, lest you forget the LORD' " (Deuteronomy 6:12); " 'Remember! Do not forget' " (Deuteronomy 9:7). Looking at the history of God's people in ancient times, seeing their mistakes and God's patient mercy, may help us to keep a more balanced perspective of the church today in this turbulent and changing world. It is in that vein that we note some of the hymns in the psalms that recount Israel's history as God's people. God wanted His people to remember how He had led them, loved them, disciplined them, preserved them, forgiven them, and blessed them. In spite of their failures and flaws, He had not forsaken them. Three great national hymns—Psalm 78, Psalm 105, and Psalm 106—review the history of Israel as God led them out of Egypt, through the wilderness, and into the Promised Land. These psalms were to be sung by God's people to keep vivid in their hearts what God had done for them in the past.

Psalm 78 highlights God's care and mercies to Israel in their sojourn from Egypt and onward (see verses 12–16). He gave them manna as one of His acts of grace, yet they still craved the flesh pots of Egypt (see verses 18–29). His chastising mercies preserved them from self-destruction (see verses 30–34). The psalmist sings of the long-suffering mercies of God: "For He remembered that they were but flesh" (verse 39). "What a God! What a people! How glorious in grace the One! How sunk in sin the other! How low must mercy condescend in helping such a people?"[6]

Psalm 105 is titled "Remember, God Keeps His Promises."[7] The song begins with a call to "give thanks to the LORD!" (verse 1), to "sing psalms to Him" (verse 2), and to "glory in His holy name" (verse 3). The psalm reminds Israel that God "remembers His covenant forever" (verse 8). It then rehearses the story of Joseph and how Israel eventually came to Egypt (see verses 13–22), as well as how the Lord delivered them from Egyptian bondage (see verses 26–38). God had remembered His promise to Abraham. He fulfilled His promise to His chosen people "that they might observe His statutes and keep His laws" (verse 45). (The first fifteen verses of this hymn are also recorded in 1 Chronicles 16:8–22, which David composed for the ceremony of moving and enshrining the ark in Jerusalem.)

The psalm ends with the Hebrew word *Hallelujah,* "Praise the Lord!" (verse 45).

Psalm 106 also begins and ends with the Hebrew word *Hallelujah!* Sandwiched between these two declarations of praise are admissions of failures, outright disobedience, and wicked idolatry. Yet in spite of all that, God did not give up on His people, but "many times He delivered them. . . . [And] He regarded their affliction . . . [and] remembered His covenant" (verses 43–45). What a wonderful, compassionate God! *Hallelujah!*

What can these psalms teach us today? We need to review our history, as individuals and as a church. Looking back over our own failures and mistakes should give us compassion for those who are still struggling with sin and compromise. Rather than criticizing, we can be encouragers and role models to those who are weak and tempted. We must take courage—and talk courage—as we look to our Divine Leader for care and direction in our future, just as He has cared for us and directed us in the past. We can make our journey toward the kingdom more joyful and pleasant by singing the great hymns that celebrate God's leading in the past:

O God, our help in ages past,
Our hope for years to come,

Our shelter from the stormy blast,
And our eternal home!

Before the hills in order stood,
Or earth received her frame,
From everlasting Thou art God,
To endless years the same.

O God, our help in ages past,
Our hope for years to come;
Be Thou our guide while life shall last,
And our eternal home![8]

The psalms often talk about singing a new song: "Sing a new song of praise to him" (Psalm 33:3, NLT). "He has given me a new song to sing, a hymn of praise to our God" (Psalm 40:3, NLT). "Sing a new song to the LORD" (Psalm 96:1, NLT). A new song titled "Ancient Words" reminds us that we find our strength and hope "in Christ alone." He is our "Cornerstone, our Comforter, our all in all."[9]

Our songs are to be sung to the Lord; He alone is worthy of our praise and worship. There are hundreds of references in Scripture that indicate or imply that our songs are to be directed to God. The songs we sing to Him, whether old or new, should be appropriate to His holiness and majesty in *both the words and the music.* We should ask ourselves of every song we sing to Him in worship, Does this song or hymn honor God? Or is it calling attention to the worshiper or to some other person or idea?

In his book, *The Music of Heaven,* John Thurber, well-known former King's Heralds quartet member, shares a personal experience that illustrates the power of music for good or ill on the human heart. His college quartet was on its way to Asheville, North Carolina, where the quartet was to sing at a youth congress. Learning that there was to be a gospel sing in the Asheville civic auditorium, the quartet members decided to stop and listen; perhaps they could get some new ideas or songs. Assuming that they were another group of performers for the event, the hostess directed them to the stage door. However, as the first group sang, Thurber's group became uncomfortable, wondering if they were in the wrong place! The last number of the first group to perform was titled "Hallelujah Boogie." The emcee then introduced Thurber's quartet. They sang a simple rendition of "The Old Rugged Cross." There was little applause. They sang another song and ended with "The Song of Heaven and Homeland." There was silence, and they quickly exited. Then as the emcee began introducing the next group, the audience indicated by lightly applauding that they wanted to hear more from this college quartet. The group sang for another twenty minutes. As they left, one of the other performers said to them, "Keep singing like this; your music is of God. I know some of our music doesn't please Him." Thurber ends his story by emphasizing that it wasn't the quartet's talent, but the songs they sang that touched hearts and uplifted Christ. There is a vast difference between singing to the glory of God to reach hearts and singing for the benefit of the musicians and/or for the purpose of entertaining the audience.[10]

Zion: City of the Great King

"Beautiful in elevation, the joy of the whole earth, is Mount Zion . . . , city of the great King" (Psalm 48:2). "The LORD has chosen Zion" (Psalm 132:13); "The LORD loves the gates of Zion" (Psalm 87:2); He has "mercy on Zion" (Psalm 102:13); "God will save Zion" (Psalm 69:35); and He has "commanded the blessing—life forevermore" upon Zion (Psalm 133:3). Zion is mentioned in at least thirty-seven of the 150 psalms. What or where is Zion?

Mount Zion and Mount Moriah, on which the temple was built, are part of the same ridge in the northern part of Jerusalem. Together, both are known as a single entity—Mount Zion. The temple itself was sometimes referred to as Mount Zion. The congregation of Israel—God's covenant people—are referred to in Scripture as Zion. Perhaps most important of all, Zion symbolizes the city of God, the New Jerusalem, where God will dwell with His people and where Christ will reign as their King.

Psalm 2, one of the great Messianic psalms, describes the nations raging and "the kings of the earth [setting] themselves . . . against the LORD and against His Anointed" (verses 2). God then declares, " ' "You are My Son, today I have begotten You. Ask of Me, and I will give You the nations for Your inheritance, and the ends of the earth for Your possession" ' " (verses 7, 8). The psalm ends with an appeal and a promise: "Kiss the Son, lest He be angry, and you perish in the way. . . . Blessed are all those who put their trust in Him" (verse 12).

In Hebrews 12, Paul encourages Christians to "endure chastening," to "pursue peace" and holiness (verses 7, 14). He then refers to the history of Israel and those who did not take hold of God's promises. He reminds his readers that they, too, have come to Mount Zion, "city of the living God, the heavenly Jerusalem . . . to the general assembly and church of the firstborn" (verses 22, 23). Paul makes it clear here that Mount Zion is the city of God, the heavenly Jerusalem. He also implies that Zion is the church, God's people who have been born again and whose names are registered in heaven. Furthermore, they have accepted the new covenant Mediator, whose blood speaks of better things than the blood of animals in the old covenant ever could.

So what are the "songs of Zion"? They are songs that exalt the Lord Jesus Christ, His saving grace, and His work as our Mediator. They are songs that remind us of our need for repentance and forgiveness. These songs encourage us along the journey to our heavenly home, Jerusalem, the city of God. They are songs that exalt our Great King and that see His church as His covenant people who strengthen their covenant relationship with Him.

James and Ellen White loved to sing. In her correspondence to friends, Ellen White frequently encouraged them "to sing the songs of Zion" in order to cheer their hearts along the way, to deflect their thoughts from petty annoyances or inconveniences, and to counteract impatient or fretful complaining.

As part of the worship experience, the songs of Zion may deepen our love for our God and fix our minds on that heavenly city to which we look forward, especially when the path is dark with the burdens of this life. So why not sing the songs of Zion, not just in corporate worship but in the daily journey to cheer our own hearts as well as the hearts of others?

We're marching to Zion,
Beautiful, beautiful Zion . . .
Beautiful city of God.[11]

O Zion, haste, thy mission high fulfilling,
To tell to all the world that God is light. . . .

Publish glad tidings, tidings of peace,
Tidings of Jesus, redemption and release.[12]

---

1. Paul Lee Tan, *Book of Illustrations* (Rockville, Md.: Assurance Publishers, n.d.), 1467.

2. Nichol, ed., *The Seventh-day Adventist Bible Commentary,* 3:639.

3. See White, *Selected Messages,* 1:344.

4. Russell Baker, quoted in Robert Spangler, *First Things First,* 16.

5. Ellen G. White, *Life Sketches of Ellen G. White* (Mountain View, Calif.: Pacific Press®, 1943), 196.

6. Andrew A. Bonar, *Christ and His Church in the Book of Psalms* (Grand Rapids, Mich.: Kregel Publications, 1978), 235.

7. As printed in the King James Version, The Open Bible, expanded ed. (Nashville: Thomas Nelson Publishers, 1983).

8. Isaac Watts, "O God, Our Help in Ages Past," in *Seventh-day Adventist Church Hymnal* (Hagerstown, Md.: Review and Herald®, 1985), no. 103.

9. Lynn DeShazo, "Ancient Words" (Mobile, Ala.: Integrity's Hosanna! Music, 2001).

10. John Thurber and Cari Haus, *The Music of Heaven* (Coldwater, Mich.: Remnant Publications, 2001), 117–119.

11. Isaac Watts, "Marching to Zion," in *Seventh-day Adventist Church Hymnal,* no. 422.

12. Mary A. Thomson, "O Zion Haste," in *Seventh-day Adventist Church Hymnal,* no. 365.

CHAPTER 8

When Worship Becomes Skewed

To understand the Israelite's illicit love affair with Baal worship, we need first to take a look at their early attraction to this heathen god when they were on the very borders of the Promised Land. Israel had conquered the Amorites, which meant obtaining some of the territory of the Moabites. Balak, the king of Moab, was terrified by the approach of this people who " 'cover the face of the earth, and are settling next to me!' " (Numbers 22:5). Balak appealed to Balaam, once a prophet of God, to come and help him by cursing Israel. Balaam knew better, but the offered reward and his pride overruled his better judgment and his knowledge of God. After repeated failed attempts to curse Israel, he left without his reward.

Balaam understood that no harm could come to Israel as long as the people were loyal to God. So he returned to Moab and proposed a new plan to bring a curse on Israel (see Numbers 31:16). The plan worked! The Moabites began inviting the people of Israel to their licentious worship orgies, "and the people began to commit harlotry with the women of Moab" (Numbers 25:1). The next step was to invite the Israelites to their sacrifices. The children of Israel joined the Moabites and "bowed down to their gods" (verse 2). Imagine the excuses they might have given to Moses. "Well, aren't we supposed to witness to our heathen neighbors? How can we reach them if we don't socialize with them?" One step leads to another! Israel had taken the fateful step of fraternizing with the enemy, and that led to the skewing—the distorting, the twisting—of their worship experience.

God has given clear instructions on how we are to relate to Him, especially in worship. As noted in chapter 2, God made it very plain to His people that they must worship Him and Him alone—no other gods, no idols, no images. However, sinful human nature tends to forget!

The dividing of the kingdom

Even King Solomon, the son of David, forgot all too quickly the clear instructions God had given to Moses, should the people choose a king: " 'Neither shall he multiply wives for himself, lest his heart turn away' " (Deuteronomy 17:17). Solomon rationalized his alliance with a pharaoh's daughter for political reasons as a means to spread the knowledge of God to heathen peoples. Yet, the influence ran the opposite direction! Solomon's heathen wives exerted such a powerful influence on him that he actually built altars and temples to their heathen gods! One compromise led to another, and gradually Solomon forgot the Source of his strength, so that he himself didn't seem to realize that he was selling out his integrity.

He built shrines in honor of Ashtoreth and Molech, a type of Baal, who required cruel child sacrifices. Though Solomon later repented, the evil influence of his example and its fallout eventually led to the dividing of the kingdom. Rehoboam, his son, rejected the sound counsel of his father's advisors and followed the evil advice of his peers. The ten northern tribes rebelled against the king, and called Jeroboam, a former servant of Solomon, to become their king (see 1 Kings 11).

Jeroboam

Jeroboam had the potential to lead Israel in the right way. Instead, in bold defiance of the God of heaven, he plunged the nation deep into apostasy and idolatry. The new king lived in fear that his subjects might, at some point, return their allegiance to the king at Jerusalem. So he determined that he would set up two new places of worship at Dan and Bethel to discourage his subjects from returning to Jerusalem.[1] He made two calves of gold, saying to the people, " 'Here are your gods, O Israel, which brought you up from the land of Egypt!' " (1 Kings 12:28). These were the very words that the mixed multitude had spoken regarding Aaron's golden calf at the foot of Mount Sinai. There are indications that Jeroboam was subtly suggesting that the people were still worshiping the true God in a new "Baal style." Archaeologists have found pieces of pottery with the words *Yahweh is Baal,* suggesting that the Israelites were attempting to synchronize the two religions.[2]

Jeroboam set apart priests from "the common people—those who were not from the priestly tribe of Levi" (verse 31, NLT) and ordained feasts similar to the feasts at Jerusalem. He included familiar aspects of worship that would make the people feel comfortable, but he mingled with them new forms of worship on a strange altar, which he hoped would appeal to the people's imagination. Alarmed by this turn of events, some of the Israelites, especially the Levites, fled to Jerusalem where they might worship God properly.

One day a prophet from Judah came to Bethel and confronted Jeroboam as he stood by the altar offering incense. The prophet predicted the birth of Josiah, who would be born to the house of David. King Josiah, he said, would burn the bones of those who now were sacrificing on the high places; they would be punished for their high-handed presumption in leading Israel away from the worship of God to the Baal-like worship of idolatry. The Bethel altar split apart as a sign of the prophecy's certainty (see 1 Kings 13:2–6). Nearly three centuries later, Judah's King Josiah fulfilled that prophecy (see 2 Kings 23:15–19).

In this incident, God gave Jeroboam an opportunity to repent and change his course. Instead of responding, however, he hardened his heart and intensified his efforts to turn his people away from the true worship of Jehovah. Throughout the record of the kings of Israel, a phrase is frequently repeated: "Jeroboam, who sinned and who made Israel sin" (1 Kings 14:16).[3] What a legacy for evil this man left for posterity!

Ahab and Jezebel

During the forty-year reign of King Asa in the southern kingdom of Judah, Israel's throne, in the north, was the center of turbulence and bloodshed. Finally, Ahab, son of Omri who founded Samaria, became king and married Jezebel, "the daughter of Ethbaal, king of the Sidonians" (1 Kings 16:31). Together, these two Baal devotees led Israel even deeper into Baal worship, establishing "high places"—Baal altars—in the capital city and throughout the realm.

Though the name *Baal* is used as "lord," it actually means "possessor" or "owner." The Baal gods took many forms, such as the god of rain, the god of fertility, etc. Baal worship was common in Canaan and in other agricultural cultures as well. It is interesting to note that Baal, as lord of the forces of nature necessary to sustain life, was the devil's substitute god for the Creator God who made all things and who sustains all life.

The religious orgies of Baal were celebrated with drunkenness, revelry, promiscuous sex, sensuality, and even child sacrifices—all under the umbrella of worship! One writer has suggested that child sacrifices were the way the Baal cult dealt with the unwanted children born from their sensual orgies, much like abortion serves our promiscuous society today.[4] "Now Ahab . . . did evil in the sight of the LORD, more than all who were before him. . . . Ahab did more to provoke the LORD God of Israel to anger than all the kings of Israel who were before him" (1 Kings 16:30, 33). Under the evil influence of Ahab and Jezebel, Israel plunged deeper and lower into the grossest forms of heathen idolatry, giving themselves up to the "intoxicating, degrading pleasures of a sensual worship. In their blind folly they chose to reject God and His worship. . . . Israel had voluntarily separated herself from Jehovah."[5] God's mercy is not easily exhausted. Through appeals and judgments He gives opportunity for His people to repent. God was about to send to Israel one of the greatest of all the prophets. Never had His people fallen so low, yet a compassionate God still yearned to reach out and save them as individuals and as a nation in spite of their fallen condition. Would His people heed the warning? Would the terrible spell of Baal worship be broken? This loving God was about to do something special, something that would go down in history as a high-water mark of God's great love for lost sinners!

Elijah the Tishbite

Without any introduction, except a statement of where he lived, without fanfare or even any credentials, the prophet Elijah suddenly appeared on the scene—at the royal palace—and announced to Ahab, " 'As surely as the LORD, the God of Israel, lives—the God I serve—there will be no dew or rain during the next few years until I give the word!' " (1 Kings 17:1, NLT). Heaven's fiat had gone forth. This message struck like a thunderbolt, an omen of divine judgment to come. "The apostasy of Israel was an evil more dreadful than all the multiplied horrors of famine."[6] Now Ahab and all Israel would know who controls the rain and the sun. Then, just as quickly as he had appeared, Elijah was gone, on his way to the brook Cherith where the Lord would sustain him during the terrible three years of drought.

Elijah was humble but fearless. He was a man of faith and lived in close fellowship with his God. We know almost nothing about his background or his life, except that he was devoted to the work of reform among his people as he saw the rapid spread of apostasy and the terrible inroads that idolatry had made among them. Overwhelmed with sorrow at what was happening, he prayed earnestly that God would somehow intervene and bring His people to repentance.

Near the end of the three years of drought, the word of the Lord came to Elijah again. " 'Go, present yourself to Ahab' " (1 Kings 18:1). Elijah tells King Ahab, "Gather all the people of Israel and bring the four hundred and fifty prophets of Baal and the four hundred prophets of Asherah who eat at Jezebel's table, and meet me at Mount Carmel" (see verse 19).

There is no more discussion, no arguments, no bargaining. Ahab fears this man, for his prayers have kept the rain and even the dew from the land for three years. The record simply states, "So Ahab sent for all the children of Israel, and gathered the prophets together on Mount Carmel" (verse 20).

On Mount Carmel

Before the drought, Mount Carmel, with its refreshing streams and flourishing groves, was a place of beauty. Now the altars of Baal stood in leafless groves under the withering curse of the prophet. Not far away was the broken-down altar of Jehovah. The heights of Carmel could be seen from many parts of the kingdom. No doubt, Elijah chose this place because of its elevation as an ideal place for the power of God to be demonstrated.

Imagine Mount Carmel on the designated day. The hosts of the people of Israel begin to arrive, wondering what this day will hold. Undoubtedly some of them are having twinges of conscience because of their apostasy. Others are possibly hoping that Elijah's efforts will be successful and that God will be honored above Baal. The prophets of Ahab and Jezebel march up in regal array. The king arrives and takes his place at the head of the Baal priests, who seem apprehensive, because Baal has not had power to overcome the prophet Elijah's mandated drought. They sense that something fearful is about to happen.

Then Elijah stands before the crowd and preaches one of the shortest sermons recorded in Scripture: " 'How long will you falter between two opinions? If the LORD is God, follow Him; but if Baal, follow him' " (verse 21).

There is a deathly silence. "The people answered him not a word" (verse 21). Elijah continues. He points out that he alone is left as a prophet of the Lord. He challenges Baal's prophets to offer a bull as a sacrifice and proposes a showdown. " 'Then you call on the name of your gods, and I will call on the name of the LORD; and the God who answers by fire, He is God' " (verse 24).

Elijah generously allows the prophets of Baal to make the first sacrifice. From morning till noon, they cry out to Baal, begging him to hear them. No fire! They leap on the altar; they cut themselves and shout incantations to try to awaken their sleeping god. The day wears on, but there is no answer! Finally, at the time of the evening sacrifice, Elijah calls the people to come near to him. He rebuilds the broken-down altar of God, which has been neglected for so many years. He digs a trench around it. He places wood on top of the altar and pours water over the wood—not once, but three times. The altar and the sacrifice are drenched. Water fills the trench around the altar. Then Elijah prays in simple tones: " 'LORD God of Abraham, Isaac, and Israel, let it be known this day that You are God in Israel. . . . Hear me, O LORD, hear me, that this people may know that You are the LORD God, and that You have turned their hearts back to You again' " (verses 36, 37).

Almost instantly, the fire of the Lord falls and consumes the sacrifice, along with the soaked wood, the stones of the altar and the dust, and even "lick[s] up the water . . . in the trench" (verse 38). The fire reminds the people of the Pillar of fire that saved their forefathers at the Red Sea. The crowd looks on in breathless anticipation at what this Great God of Israel has done. They fall on their faces in awe and wonder, crying out, " 'The LORD, He is God! The LORD, He is God!' " (verse 39).

"Behold I will send you Elijah the prophet"

The Old Testament ends with the encouraging prophecy: " 'Behold, I will send you Elijah the prophet before the coming of the great and dreadful day of the LORD. And he will turn the hearts of the fathers to the children, and the hearts of the children to their fathers' " (Malachi 4:5, 6). Jesus declared of John the Baptist, " 'If you are willing to receive it, he is Elijah who is to come' " (Matthew 11:14; cf. Luke 1:13–17). Malachi's prophecy is also applicable to the second coming of Christ. Is there an Elijah voice for today? Is there an Elijah message for earth's last crisis? Is there anyone who is preaching a warning against the Baals of our day? Is anyone calling for reformation and a turning back to God? The answer is a resounding Yes! God does have an "Elijah" for this corrupt, Baal-worshiping age. He does have a prophetic people who are proclaiming the everlasting gospel to the whole world. " 'Fear God and give glory to Him . . . worship Him who made heaven and earth' " (Revelation 14:7). They are warning that " 'Babylon is fallen' " (verse 8) and that God's people are to come out of Babylon—or Baal worship (see Revelation 18:1–4). Finally, they are sounding the alarm that those who participate in any kind of false worship, whether worship of the beast or of Baal or of any false god, will be subject to God's wrath against all man-made worship that does not recognize Him as the one and only Creator God. Thank God there is an "Elijah" people today! We have the privilege of being instruments in God's hand to sound the warning and give the invitation to turn away from the false gods and worship the true God!

We become like what we worship. God warns us not to worship the gods of this world, because they lead us to destruction. If we are to become like our wonderful Creator God, we must worship Him and Him alone!

Modern Baal worship

What are some of the false gods that are so popular in our world today? Many Baals confront us in this postmodern world—materialism, secularism, self-worship, indulgence, and hedonistic idolatry! Less obvious, however, is the increasing popularity of a whole new approach to religion, known as the emerging church. It is not a new theology; rather, it is a coming together of both old and new attitudes, views, liturgies, and styles of worship. According to this thinking, one's beliefs are not a test. Rather your tastes, desires, and lifestyle may determine how you live and how you worship. There is no distinction between good and evil, between secular and sacred! Multitudes are being drawn to this "anything goes" type of religion, which cuts across denominational lines and beliefs.

However, there is an even more sinister and dangerous "Baal" out there today, which is gaining popularity. It is a Baal god with multitudes of devotees—and growing! They can be found in ordinary churches, in séances, in small groups of sophisticated young intellectuals, in gymnasiums, in seminar rooms, or even in Christian churches. You will find the children of these devotees reading the Harry Potter books religiously!

With all of his intelligence and his millennia of experience, Lucifer has pulled out all the stops in these last days of earth's history to deceive the human race, even the "very elect" if possible, in order to sell the world on his new "Baal" god! This new god is more sophisticated than all his previous Baals! In Satan's effort to entice the postmodern mind, including Christians, he calls his Baal the New Age!

Many Christians are not aware that New Age thinking has infiltrated their churches. The movement is subtle, using Christian words and expressions to hide its true identity. It appeals to the intellect, but more important, it is essentially ego-worship, using the "higher self" as its revealed god.

In his book, *Deceived by the New Age,* Will Baron writes of his journey from growing up in a Christian home to becoming enchanted with mysticism, psychic powers, channeling, and the promise of finding his "higher self." He was especially devoted to one of the Eastern masters. Imagine then, his shock one day to hear his mentor suggest that they should now give their allegiance, not to the masters, but to Jesus. Not only that, but they were to attend Christian churches, get acquainted with the members, use Christian lingo, and infiltrate the churches with New Age concepts. Eventually, Will Baron heard about the writings of Ellen White and found one of her books in a public library. When he read her description of Satan, he was stunned and shaken, because it described in detail the person he had been talking with in his encounters—the person he thought was Jesus! This was the turning point for Will Baron. Now, instead of preaching New Age at the beach, he seeks to warn people of the dangers inherent in these teachings.[7]

Ray Yungen has written a book on the inroads that New Age teachings are making in various levels of our society. Names such as Robert Schuller and Norman Vincent Peale have helped to popularize the tenants of the New Age movement. Many of these concepts are being taught in popular seminars to business people. One New Age teacher commented, "All I have to do is drop the mystical connotations, and businessmen eat this stuff up."[8]

Someone has estimated that no less than 20 percent of the U.S. population (forty million people) are sympathetic to New Age ideas.[9] The goal of the New Age movement is to "merge these practices into society so that they will be considered normal and acceptable."[10] For example, the word *meditation* is a buzzword in New Age lingo. Biblical meditation is for the purpose of focusing on God's Word as He has given it. New Age meditation is clearing the mind of all thoughts, so that another power can take control. Another example: the New Age movement defends the practice of "centering down" as good for Christians, but it is akin to self-hypnosis.

God has given us His Word and the modern gift of prophecy. He has given warnings regarding the dangers of false gods and false worship. "As spiritualism more closely imitates the nominal Christianity of the day, it has greater power to deceive and ensnare. . . . [Satan] will appear [as] . . . an angel of light. . . . Many undeniable wonders will be performed."[11]

We are living in the most solemn and dangerous period of earth's history. God has given to His last-day church the Elijah message for this final hour. We dare not fail to give it clearly and emphatically! We dare not skew the worship of our God by compromising and adopting the popular cultural and entertainment styles of worship, thus substituting the worship of a Holy God with the Baal worship of our society.

Three fatal steps to Baal worship

There are three fatal steps to Baal worship, which Israel followed and of which we must beware: First, Israel's fall into Baal worship did not happen suddenly. It was a slow, gradual departure from the Lord, followed by a faster slide into Baal territory, gaining momentum as the people went deeper into its evil worship.

The second step was compromise with the enemy. Compromise may seem insignificant at first, but every step in the wrong direction deepens the ties with wrong and increases our distance from God.

Third, was infiltration into the camp of the enemy. This is one of Satan's favorite tools. At first, just a few Israelites ventured into Baal territory. Then, they in turn enticed others, and eventually, Baal actually became the norm for Israel's worship. On Mount Carmel, when Elijah asked for those who were on the Lord's side to take a stand, no one said a word. The Baal deception had blinded their eyes to truth.

There is only one sure protection against falling for Baal worship, and that is to be firmly protected by God's divine security system—His Word! There is only one safety net for those who have fallen for Baal worship, and that is a genuine, saving relationship with the Lord Jesus Christ. Individually and as a church, we must have a Mount Carmel experience, a revival of true godliness. Then we must share the good news of the gospel—by personal testimony, in mission work in foreign lands, in churches and evangelistic halls, by satellite, on the Internet, to our neighbors! In whatever way we can, we must share the good news that God loves His children and wants them to escape the enemy's snares and be saved for His kingdom. That is the Elijah message! That is our work for these last days! May we not disappoint our wonderful God who loves us and has done so much to redeem us and protect us from evil and destruction! "God calls for men [and women] like Elijah . . . men who will bear His message with faithfulness, regardless of the consequences; men who will speak the truth bravely, though it call for the sacrifice of all they have."[12]

---

1. See White, *Prophets and Kings*, 99–101.

2. William G. Dever, *Did God Have a Wife?* (Grand Rapids, Mich.: Eerdmans, 2005), 131, 133, 162–167.

3. According to some estimates, this phrase appears about fifty times in Scripture.

4. See Jay Johansen, "Baal Worship: A Consistent Religion," Pregnant Pause, accessed January 19, 2011, www.pregnantpause.org/poetry/baal.htm; Morris Jastrow Jr., J. Frederic McCurdy, and Duncan B. McDonald, "Ba'al and Ba'al Worship," Jewish Encyclopedia, accessed January 19, 2011, www.jewishencyclopedia.com/view.jsp?letter=B&artid=2.

5. White, *Prophets and Kings*, 116.

6. Ibid., 127.

7. See Will Baron, *Deceived by the New Age* (Nampa, Idaho: Pacific Press®, 1990).

8. Ray Yungen, *For Many Shall Come in My Name* (Silverton, Ore.: Lighthouse Trails Publishing, 2007), 39.

9. Robert Fuller, *Spiritual but Not Religious* (Oxford: Oxford University Press, 2001), 99.

10. Yungen, *For Many Shall Come in My Name*, 38.

11. Ellen G. White, *The Great Controversy* (Mountain View, Calif.: Pacific Press®, 1950), 588.

12. White, *Prophets and Kings*, 142.

CHAPTER 9

Worship: Counterfeit or Genuine?

In November 2009, a White House photographer captured a scene that made headlines: Michaele Salahi clasping her hands around President Obama's right hand while her smiling husband, Tareq, looks on. The couple had crashed a presidential state dinner for invited guests only. Somehow, not even the embarrassed Secret Service guards seemed to know how the couple was able to get by the checkpoints without anyone verifying that they were not on the guest list.

The Bible tells us that there is coming the grandest of all "state dinners" for invited guests only, but we can be sure that the angel security guards of the King who has invited us will not make any mistakes. In fact, our King knows who are His genuine followers and who are mere "pretense worshipers," although it is difficult, if not impossible, for us to detect the difference. In this chapter we will look at what the biblical prophets had to say about pretense worship in their time, and more important, what God considers to be the genuine qualities of true worship.

Messages to Israel from Hosea

In spite of Elijah's reform in Israel, wicked King Ahab continued to exert his evil influence on his people. But God is merciful, and He frequently sent prophets to appeal to the people to return to Him. God doesn't just use words; He sometimes uses the lives of the prophets to appeal to His people to "get real" in worshiping Him. Hosea's acted-out prophecy is one of the most poignant in all of Scripture. Hosea's wife was unfaithful to him at some point; scholars are not agreed on the sequence of events in the book. God used Hosea's tragedy to illustrate His heartbreak over His people's unfaithfulness.

The ten tribes had gone deep into idolatry and its accompanying evils. God said He would punish those who " 'burned incense' " to Baal, who adorned their bodies with " 'earrings and jewelry,' " following their false spiritual lovers and forgetting Him (Hosea 2:13). Like Hosea's wife, Israel had committed spiritual harlotry; yet God was eager to take the Israelites back if only they would return to Him! Once more, God patiently called them to return to the One they claimed to worship but to whom they had been unfaithful. Hosea warned them in the words of God, " 'My people are destroyed for lack of knowledge' " (Hosea 4:6). God pleaded with them in tender love language: " 'How can I give you up . . . ? How can I hand you over, Israel? . . . My heart churns within Me; My sympathy is stirred' " (Hosea 11:8). Hosea ends his appeal from God with great pathos: "O Israel, return to the LORD your God. . . . 'I will heal . . . [your] backsliding, I will love . . . [you] freely, for My anger has turned away' " (Hosea 14:1, 4).

Amos the sheep herder

Amos, a contemporary of Hosea and a prophet in Judah, was sent to Bethel, Israel's center of idolatry, to warn the people of judgment to come. Amos, a farmer, likens the people to summer fruit; he sees them, like fruit, spoiling all too quickly (see Amos 8:1–4). They have a form of worship, but it is not acceptable to God! Their religion, like their worship, is superficial; it salves the conscience, but it is not genuine! For example, they professed to keep the Sabbath. Yet they waited at the gates of the city on Sabbath evening and asked, "When does the sun go down, so we can sell our wheat?" They falsified their balances with deceit and took advantage of the poor (see Amos 8:5, 6).

Amos does not mince words: "Woe to you who desire the day of the LORD! For what good is the day of the LORD to you? It will be darkness, and not light. It will be as though a man fled from a lion, and a bear met him!" (Amos 5:18, 19). Furthermore, says God through the prophet, " 'Behold the days are coming . . . that I will send a famine on the land, not a famine of bread, nor a thirst for water, but of hearing the words of the LORD' " (Amos 8:11). When God stops calling us, we are in deep trouble! God through the prophet appeals to Israel, " 'Seek Me and live' " (Amos 5:4). He warns them not to worship at Bethel, Gilgal, or Beersheba—all places of the blended worship of Yahweh and Baal (see Amos 5:5, 6).

God reminds them that He despises their feast days and their sacred assemblies. That He will not accept their grain offerings (see verses 21, 22). That He will not listen to " 'the noise of . . . [their] songs' " (verse 23). *What does God want from them?* " 'Let justice run down like water, and righteousness like a mighty stream' " (verse 24). As we will see again in the writings of the other Old Testament prophets, this is God's passion: *do righteousness*, don't just profess it or talk about it. *Live by justice and mercy*—that to God is better than mere talk or profession! God wants our hearts, not our pretense worship!

Amos ends his prophecy to the people of Israel by portraying their restoration, when God will " 'bring back the captives of . . . [His] people Israel' " and " 'will plant them in their land' " (Amos 9:14, 15). What a gracious God! Always ready to forgive, to restore, and to reestablish Israel in the land He has promised to all of His faithful children!

Micah, prophet to Judah

Micah was a younger contemporary of Hosea and Isaiah and prophesied in Judah during the latter part of the eighth century B.C. when Assyria was the dominant power in the area. Ahaz, during his time as king of Judah, went the full length of idolatry and even "burned his children in the fire, according to the abominations of the nations whom the LORD had cast out" (2 Chronicles 28:3). The traditional forms of worship were still practiced, while at the same time they were combined with idolatrous heathen rituals.

Ahaz was succeeded by his son, Hezekiah, who "did what was right in the sight of the LORD" (2 Chronicles 29:2) and sought to undo the apostasy his father had led, to abolish idolatry, and to bring reform, both spiritual and moral, among his people. His objective was to bring his people back to the worship of the true God.[1]

Hezekiah began his reign by opening the house of the Lord, making repairs, and restoring the temple worship. He destroyed the heathen altars in Jerusalem and reinstated the Passover service. The record states that "there was great joy in Jerusalem," because nothing like this had happened since the days of Solomon (2 Chronicles 30:26).

Micah suggests that Judah's "wounds are incurable" (Micah 1:9), because this nation has followed in the footsteps of their northern neighbor, Israel, in idolatrous worship. He also describes some of the social evils that his people are practicing and the judgments that are determined upon the princes and prophets. He looks forward to the restoration of God's kingdom and prophesies the very place of the Messiah's birth and the work that He would do (see Micah 5).

Micah asks God, What do you really want from us? "What can we bring to the LORD? What kind of offerings should we give him? Should we bow before God with offerings of yearling calves? Should we offer him thousands of rams and ten thousand rivers of olive oil? Should we sacrifice our firstborn children to pay for our sins?" (Micah 6:6, 7, NLT). Micah tells the people that God has great plans for them. That He wants righteousness and that He wants them to enjoy His blessings. Then comes the bottom line: "O people, the LORD has told you what is good, and this is what He requires of you: to do what is right, to love mercy, and to walk humbly with your God" (verse 8, NLT).

God's desires for His people are simple, uncomplicated, clear, and emphatic: He wants His children to be obedient (do what is right), be good to their fellow human beings (love and show mercy to them), and walk humbly with their God (recognize Him as Creator and yourself as the creature).

It sounds easy enough, yet it is impossible for poor sinful human beings to achieve—unless they seek Him! Micah ends his message, as do most of the prophets, with hope for Israel, because of God's great love and compassion for His people. He will do miracles for them, forgive their sins, and show His great faithfulness to them (see Micah 7:14–20). Those same promises are for us today as individuals and as a church!

Isaiah on pretense worship

Isaiah begins his message to Judah by describing the nation's spiritual condition: "The whole head is sick, and the whole heart faints. . . . There is no soundness in it, but wounds and bruises and putrefying sores" (Isaiah 1:5, 6). God has had enough! He is tired of their multiple sacrifices—even the incense is " 'an abomination' " to Him (verse 13). Why is God so disgusted with their worthless offerings? Because the hands that offer them are covered with blood. No matter how many prayers they utter, He will not listen to them (see verse 15)! Does God contradict His own instructions here?

God *did* give the worship rituals to Israel, but He never intended that they become an end in themselves, substitutes for real spirituality. All too often the rituals were followed as a mere form to make the person doing them look good to others. God is not condemning their sacred meetings and feast days but the emptiness of their profession. This is what He hates—a form of religion without any genuine spiritual power! The people make a pompous show of their religion, while their spiritual life has withered, and their lives are filled with deceit and corruption. Their souls are defiled. God cannot accept such pretense worship! Even their fasting is offensive to Him, for they fast for contention, strife, and debate.

" ' "Why have we fasted . . . and You have not seen?" ' " they want to know (Isaiah 58:3). And God is quick to reply that what He wants in fasting is not sackcloth and ashes for show, not outward piety and bowing of the head, not strife and debate. Rather, He wants to see consequences from their fasting; He wants to see fasting that results in action—letting the oppressed go free, breaking the yoke of bondage, feeding the hungry, taking care of the homeless, clothing the naked, feeding the hungry, and taking care of their own! These are the fruits of the offerings, the prayers, and the fasting that will be acceptable before a Holy God (see Isaiah 58).

Isaiah spends considerable time throughout his book emphasizing God's salvation and righteousness, which would be revealed in the coming of the Messiah. He talks about the foreigner who has joined himself to the Lord, keeps the Sabbath, but then wonders if he is really part of God's people (see Isaiah 56). Isaiah emphatically answers, Yes. The foreigner (the new convert) who joins himself to the Lord, holds fast to the covenant, and keeps the Sabbath—God will make " 'joyful in . . . [His] house of prayer' " (Isaiah 56:7). God's purpose for Israel of old was that they would share the gospel with all peoples of the earth. They were to be " 'a light to the Gentiles' " (Isaiah 42:6) around them, so that they, too, might be ready to receive the Messiah when He would come. Yet, all too often Israel and Judah selfishly hoarded the blessings of God to themselves, and in so doing, the very blessings that God intended for them to share became a curse to their selfish hearts. Even their Sabbath assemblies, God said, were a burden to Him. Why? Because He said, " 'I cannot endure iniquity' " (Isaiah 1:13). What He really wanted from His people was their hearts. He offered them cleansing and new hearts! " 'Wash yourselves, . . . put away the evil of your doings. . . . Cease to do evil' " (verse 16).

Then with great pathos, God says, " 'Come now, and let us reason together . . . though your sins are like scarlet, they shall be as white as snow' " (verse 18). The results: "Arise shine; for your light has come and the glory of the LORD has risen upon you" (Isaiah 60:1).

The last few chapters of Isaiah virtually burst with promises of the glorious reign of the Messiah. Today, we have the privilege and opportunity to share the good news in ways that the people of Isaiah's time, or even those in our parent's generation, could not have imagined. Are we doing it?

Jeremiah's call to reformation

The prophet Jeremiah ministered to Judah during the last forty years before the captivity. These were difficult years. Josiah was the last good king of Judah, and Jeremiah's ministry no doubt contributed to the spiritual reforms that took place during King Josiah's reign. Early in his reign, while still a teenager, Josiah "began to seek the God of his father David" (2 Chronicles 34:3). He purged Jerusalem of idols, destroyed the pagan altars, burned the bones of Baal prophets on their own altars, and "cleansed Judah and Jerusalem" (verse 5). He repaired the temple and reinstated the Passover celebration (see 2 Chronicles 35:1–19). The revival and reformation led by Josiah was unprecedented in Judah's history. God listened to Josiah because his " ' " 'heart was tender and . . . [he] humbled . . . [himself] before God' " ' " (2 Chronicles 34:27).

Jeremiah, like Isaiah, was concerned for his people, who wanted to appear religious but whose hearts were far from God. He chided Judah for following Israel's example in " 'play[ing] the harlot' " and not turning to the Lord except in " 'pretense' " (Jeremiah 3:8, 10). For example, Jeremiah witnessed his people standing at the gates of the temple for worship, repeating the words, " ' "the temple of the LORD, the temple of the LORD" ' " (Jeremiah 7:4). Their pious words were really " 'lying words' " for they were a cover-up for stealing, adultery, false dealings, and even burning incense to Baal (verse 8). How easy it is to fall into the habit of using the proper words—religious buzzwords—as a kind of "sacred cover" that will somehow make the person look religious, while the heart is filled with secret sins. Unless they changed their ways, Jeremiah warned them, God would not accept them, no matter how pious their words (see verses 1–15)! And God insisted, " ' "*Obey* My voice, and I will be your God, and you shall be My people. And *walk* in all the ways that I have commanded you, that it may be well with you" ' " (verse 23; emphasis supplied). In these last days of earth's history, as people come to worship God, they need to hear what He is saying to them—in His Word! They need to hear the warnings and the conditions for receiving His promises!

Jeremiah predicted the reign of a righteous King who would save Judah and restore Israel. His name? " 'THE LORD OUR RIGHTEOUSNESS' " (Jeremiah 23:6). If only the people had listened to his message of hope, they could have avoided their tragic end in captivity. Jeremiah recorded the capture of Jerusalem under the evil reign of Zedekiah. Nebuchadnezzar and his Babylonian army laid siege to Jerusalem, broke down the walls, and burned the house of the Lord. They took as their booty the precious vessels, the gold and silver, back to Babylon.

Jeremiah eventually was cast into prison for his straight preaching. His message lives on. It still speaks to us today, for God's last warning message is for His people to get out of Babylon (see Jeremiah 50:8; Revelation 18:4). His call for Judah to remember their Maker is likewise echoed in God's last call to worship the Creator (see Jeremiah 51:15–19; Revelation 14:7).

Isaiah's theophany[2]

We have already looked at Isaiah's ministry and the difficulties he faced as he was called to the prophetic office. We now look at the best of Isaiah—when God confirmed His call to him in a very unique way! Few human beings have had the glorious opportunity of a theophany—an encounter in which God appears to them or discloses Himself to them in a supernatural way. The prophet Isaiah, faced with political unrest from the Assyrian hosts and the leprosy of apostasy and rebellion that afflicted his people, shrank from the seemingly hopeless task God had given him. Despair overwhelmed him! Suddenly, as he stood beneath the portico of the temple, a vision of God's glory flooded the place. Isaiah saw Yahweh sitting on a throne, high and lifted up. He saw the seraphim on either side of the throne, their faces veiled in wonder and adoration. He heard voices united in praise, saying, " 'Holy, holy, holy, is the LORD of hosts; the whole earth is full of His glory!' " (Isaiah 6:3). Awed by this triplet of holies, Isaiah was overwhelmed with the heavenly admiration and praise from the angelic hosts to the Majesty of the universe!

What a contrast! Isaiah had been focused on his people's sinful course, on the problems surrounding the nation, on his own inadequacy for his task. Now God had given him a new scene to behold—a powerful, Holy God who holds up the universe, who created this little planet, and who also had given Isaiah a work to do for Him! Suddenly, all of Isaiah's concerns seemed so small by comparison to the glory of God! Overwhelmed with awe, Isaiah must have struggled to grasp the depth of God's purity and the height of His holiness: *The whole earth is full of His glory, and I'm just now seeing it? He is holy, and I am sinful and unclean, yet I have seen Him with my own eyes. I have heard the angel choirs with my own ears! The door posts of the temple are shaking, and the house is filled with smoke.* Isaiah cries out,

" 'Woe is me, for I am undone! Because I am a man of unclean lips, and I dwell in the midst of a people of unclean lips; for my eyes have seen the King, the LORD of hosts' " (verse 5).

That response is natural when human beings truly become aware of and sense God's holiness. True humility is inspired by awe, reverence, and admiration of the divine; His holiness transcends the human grasp. Isaiah saw himself and his nation as unclean and unworthy, because he had seen the King, the Lord of hosts! Then one of the seraphim came and touched Isaiah's tongue with a live coal off the altar. His iniquity was purged, his heart was touched, and he was now ready to affirm the call of God, " 'Here am I! Send me' " (verse 8). Isaiah never forgot that encounter. His vision of God's glory and the live coal touching his lips drove him to prophesy, preach, and plead with his people for six decades, often in the face of opposition and resistance. His great prophecies of the Messiah and the final triumph of God's kingdom gave him hope and courage and a holy boldness.

Isaiah's message to his people then, and to us now, described the new heaven and new earth that God has promised to His children and that He is preparing for us. " 'And it shall come to pass that from one New Moon to another, and from one Sabbath to another, all flesh shall come to worship before Me,' says the LORD" (Isaiah 66:23).

Worship here below is our preparation for that great worship experience above! God wants true worshipers, whose hearts have been renewed by grace and whose worship comes from loyal and obedient lives. God does not want pretense worship! He wants real worship from His children, worship that comes from hearts that are in awe of Him. Hearts that beat with love and gratitude for what this wonderful and majestic God has done for us. He wants to prepare us for that heavenly worship with angels and the hosts of the redeemed. Now is our time of preparation for that event. Every day of our lives is an opportunity for us to build characters that, by His grace, will be able to stand in the presence of our Holy God! Every worship service here should be a practice session for that heavenly worship service there!

---

1. See *The Seventh-day Adventist Bible Commentary,* 4:1012.

2. *Theophany* is a transliteration of the Greek word *theophaneia,* meaning an "appearance of God." It refers to a divine disclosure or to the appearance of a deity to a human.

CHAPTER 10

The God of Second Chances

Animal shelters take in lost, abandoned, or abused animals with the hope of finding new homes for them. They are, ideally, in the business of giving second chances to these unfortunate animals. Our great and loving God is in the business of giving people second chances for the life He has planned for them. In this chapter we will see how often God reaches out to His wandering and lost children, offering them rescue, restoration, and a second chance!

Zedekiah, the last king of Judah, had been warned both by Jeremiah and Ezekiel that unless the nation repented and turned to God, it would not escape the ravages of the Babylonian armies. Zedekiah was taken captive in the first siege of Jerusalem and soon after suffered a miserable end. What would happen to Judah? Would it have a second chance?

Ezekiel's ministry

Ezekiel, prophet and priest, ministered in one of the darkest periods of Judah's history. He was taken captive to Babylon in the second siege of Jerusalem. Sometime before the siege, possibly early in his ministry, while sitting in his house with the elders of Judah, he was given a vision of God's glory and was also shown the reason for the judgments that were about to fall on Judah. "The Spirit lifted me up between earth and heaven, and brought me in visions of God to Jerusalem" (Ezekiel 8:3). There he looked into the inner court of the temple and saw "the image of jealousy" (verse 3). Whatever that image was, God made it clear to Ezekiel that " 'the great abominations that the house of Israel commits here' " were turning Him away from the people (verse 6). In vision, Ezekiel went into another area of the temple and saw "every sort of creeping thing, abominable beasts, and all the idols of the house of Israel, portrayed all around on the walls" (verse 10). These idols were probably images of heathen gods. Then Ezekiel saw seventy elders of Israel worshiping idols in a dark room, saying, " ' "The LORD does not see us, the LORD has forsaken the land" ' " (verse 12). Next, Ezekiel was shown another room where women were weeping for Tammuz, a Sumerian goddess (see verse 14). Finally, the prophet was taken to the inner court of the Lord's house and saw there twenty-five men "worshiping the sun toward the east" (verse 16). God's response to that insult was, " 'My eye will not spare nor will I have pity' " (verse 18).

Later Ezekiel was taken captive to Babylon, and from the banks of the Chebar River he gave encouragement to his fellow captives and faithfully ministered to his people.

All too soon, Nebuchadnezzar's forces defeated the Hebrew armies, took their king prisoner, and conquered the nation! Saddest of all, Solomon's temple, which had stood for some four centuries, was destroyed, burned to the ground.

Yet no matter how dark the night, God always finds a remnant of faithful ones to represent Him. Even when he was in prison in the king's court, Jeremiah continued to encourage the faithful remnant who still remained in the city. God had loyal witnesses who would represent Him to the whole nation of Babylon for many years! "Through the faithfulness of His children, God was glorified in all the earth."[1]

Daniel and his friends

Daniel was of the royal line of Judah. He and his three friends were strong, healthy, and intelligent young men who were taken captive to Babylon. They were also loyal worshipers of Yahweh and were not ashamed to declare their devotion to Him. When confronted with a menu that included meat offered to idols, the eating of which would indicate they were giving homage to the Babylonian gods, they refused. Their request to be given a more simple and healthy diet, consistent with their lifestyle and convictions, was granted and respected, as were their religious convictions! God honored the faithfulness of Daniel and his friends and blessed them with good health and the favor of the Babylonian court throughout their service there. When they were forced from their Judean homes, how could those young men have known that they were beginning a long and arduous term of mission service in heathen Babylon?

For Daniel, the call included the prophetic office. Not long after he and his friends began their service in Babylon, the king had a dream that troubled him. None of his wise men, magicians, or astrologers could tell him *what* he dreamed, much less the interpretation. In desperation, the king finally commanded that all the wise men be killed. This decree would include Daniel. Risking his life, Daniel asked for time to pray to his God for an understanding of the dream and its interpretation. The story is well known to students of Bible prophecy. God showed Daniel the king's dream and its interpretation, and Daniel gave this information to the king, making sure to let him know that his insight came from the God of heaven (see Daniel 2). The king made Daniel a ruler over the province of Babylon and also gave his friends positions in the government.

Through it all, God was working out His purposes to give the king and his heathen nation a picture of the true God of heaven. There is more! Nebuchadnezzar's dream of the great image, with its head of gold representing his kingdom, prompted him to build a ninety-feet-high statue all of gold to represent the monarch and the kingdom (see Daniel 3:1, NLT). King Nebuchadnezzar subsequently sent messages to all his officials throughout the realm to come to the Plain of Dura for the dedication service of the image. The vast crowd was then told that at the sound of musical instruments, every person must bow down before the statue of King Nebuchadnezzar. If anyone failed to do so, he would be thrown into a fiery furnace! At the appointed moment, everyone bowed down—everyone that is, except Daniel's friends, Shadrach, Meshach, and Abed-Nego!

Immediately, informants rushed to the king with the news that some Jews had refused to bow down. The young men were brought before the king. He questioned them and told them he would give them another chance. However, they made it clear to him that they would not fall down and worship his image whether or not their God saw fit to spare them from the flames. They could not and would not give their worship to anyone other than the God of heaven! The king was so furious that his face became distorted, and he commanded the furnace to be heated seven times hotter and the men to be thrown into it. The heat of the flames destroyed the soldiers who threw the three men into the furnace! Then came the surprise: suddenly, the king sees *four* men walking amid the flames! " 'And the form of the fourth,' " the king exclaimed, " 'is like the Son of God' " (Daniel 3:25).

The three Hebrew young men came out of the furnace with not even a hair of their bodies singed! The king praised their God for sending an angel to rescue these men who were willing to die rather than to serve or worship any god but their own Yahweh God! He promoted them to higher positions and decreed that no one should speak against their God (see Daniel 3:28–30)!

There are Christians today who are willing to compromise their allegiance to God for lesser threats than a fiery furnace! At what price do I estimate my loyalty to God? How much am I willing to sacrifice to be true to Him? Am I willing to lose a friend, or even a job, in order to worship Him? Am I willing to stand up for a principle of worship that is not popular in my culture? If you are not sure how you would answer these questions, take a look at the next great missionary story.

Shortly after the fall of Babylon to the Medes and Persians, Daniel faced another crisis. Darius the Mede was now on the throne. Darius chose Daniel to be one of the three governors over the satraps. Jealousy of Daniel spread among them, but they could find no pretext against him except for his religion. They finally contrived a law that no one could worship or pray to any god except King Darius for thirty days—and flattered the king into signing it! When he realized the purpose of the law was to trap Daniel, Darius regretted what he had done, but it was too late. The law could not be changed. Daniel was thrown in the lions' den, and this heathen king spent the night in fasting, unable to sleep (see Daniel 6:18). Early the next morning, Darius hurried to the lions' den and cried out, " 'Daniel, servant of the living God, has your God . . . been able to deliver you from the lions?' " (verse 20). Imagine his relief and delight—and his amazement—when he heard Daniel's voice replying, " 'My God sent His angel and shut the lions' mouths, so that they have not hurt me' " (verse 22).

The king then made a counter decree, declaring that everyone in his dominion "must tremble and fear before the God of Daniel" (verse 26). The God of heaven showed Himself strong in behalf of His prophet! Everyone in the realm now knew that this great God of the Hebrews delivers His children and gives them second chances at life!

Cyrus the Persian

Many years ago, Sherman A. Nagel, a Seventh-day Adventist leader, wrote a book, *Cyrus the Persian,* based on historical information.[2] It is an intriguing story of how the grandfather of Cyrus tried to do away with the infant when he was born, because he did not want a male heir. Through a rather lengthy series of strange and providential circumstances, the life of Cyrus was spared and he eventually came to the throne of Persia—at the very time when Jeremiah's seventy-year captivity period for the Jews was about to end. So, as the Jews saw the armies of Cyrus approaching the walls of Babylon, they took it as a sign that their long captivity must be drawing to a close.

Through Isaiah, the Lord had said, " 'He [Cyrus] shall build My city and let My exiles go free,' " (Isaiah 45:13). Daniel studied those prophecies and prayed earnestly that God would fulfill them (see Daniel 9:1–4).[3]

Again, the Jews must have reminded Cyrus of God's care for him, quoting Isaiah: " ' "That you [Cyrus] may know that I, the LORD, who call you by your name, am the God of Israel. . . . I have named you, though you have not known Me" ' " (Isaiah 45:3, 4). As Cyrus's attention was drawn to these prophecies and how God had addressed him by name, his heart was moved and he determined that he would fulfill God's mission for Him.[4]

So the Lord impressed Cyrus in the first year of his reign to make a decree that enabled the captives to return to their homeland. Furthermore, the king said, "The LORD God . . . has commanded me to build Him a house at Jerusalem which is in Judah" (Ezra 1:2). Cyrus made provision for those Jews who chose to make the trip back to Jerusalem. He also provided for the rebuilding of the temple, including returning the sacred articles from the temple, which Nebuchadnezzar had confiscated at the time of his siege of Jerusalem. Cyrus was God's instrument for Judah's second chance!

Return of the exiles

There was great rejoicing among the children of the dispersion as the news of Cyrus's decree filtered to the far reaches of the empire. About fifty thousand Jews responded to the opportunity to return to their own land. In addition, friends and neighbors gave gifts of gold and other precious things for the work of rebuilding the temple (see verses 5–11). Zerubbabel, a descendant of King David, and Jeshua, the high priest, were given the responsibility of leading the exiles after their return to Judea. According to Ezra, one of the first things the exiles did when they returned was to build an altar near the temple site and offer burnt offerings to God according to the Law of Moses (see Ezra 3:2, 3). They reinstated the Feast of Tabernacles and other appointed feasts. The people began raising funds for the masons and carpenters. Within a year of their arrival, they began the work of laying the foundation for the new temple. Notice Ezra's description: "When the builders laid the foundation of the temple of the LORD, the priests stood in their apparel with trumpets . . . to praise the LORD. . . . And they sang responsively, praising and giving thanks to the LORD" (Ezra 3:10, 11).

When the exiles returned from their captivity, they made first things first—their religious worship to God was a priority above all else. They were grateful for this second chance and made God's honor first!

Refusing unwanted help

The enemy of God is never satisfied when things go well. Ezra records that as the work was progressing, some of their Samaritan neighbors offered to help them build the temple on the pretext that they, too, were worshipers of God. When their help was refused, they began making trouble and tried to frustrate plans for rebuilding the temple. Had the Jewish leaders accepted their offer of help, they would have opened the door to the idolatry of the Samaritans with their long history of compromised worship. Speaking of the nations around them, God had earlier warned Israel, " 'Make no covenant with them' " (Deuteronomy 7:2).

At one point, while Nehemiah was building the wall, Sanballat and Geshem sent for him to meet with them. Nehemiah's answer was quick and pointed. " 'I am doing a great work, so that I cannot come down. Why should the work cease while I leave it and go down to you?' " (Nehemiah 6:3).

God's people need that kind of courage and determination today. We dare not compromise with those who claim to be His followers but who do not keep His commandments and are not committed to His covenant. "Like Nehemiah, God's people are neither to fear nor to despise their enemies. Putting their trust in God, they are to go steadily forward, doing His work . . . and committing to His providence the cause for which they stand."[5] The outcome of the Samaritan encounter was a slowing down of the work of rebuilding the temple, and discouragement among the Jews ensued.

The prophets of God helping them

When the first exiles returned, they were filled with joy and determination to make the building of God's house their priority. Now discouragement set in, and they found it easier to make their own interests first, rather than fight with their Samaritan neighbors. They built nice homes for themselves, while the work of building the temple was neglected. God's blessings were removed while they murmured and complained. They needed to learn that if they desired God's blessings, they must put His interests first in their lives. So, God in His mercy sent them prophets to help them gain a right perspective, a second chance.

Haggai began his message to Judah by reminding the people that they were dwelling in " 'paneled houses,' " while God's temple lay in ruins (Haggai 1:4). God's house " 'is in ruins, while every one of you runs to his own house' " (verse 9). Yet Haggai assured them of God's presence among them. "So the LORD stirred up the spirit of Zerubbabel . . . and the spirit of all the remnant of the people; and they came and worked on the house of the LORD" (verse 14). They "rose up and began to build the house of God . . . and the prophets of God were with them, helping them" (Ezra 5:2).

Another problem arose when the foundation for the temple had been completed. As the people were rejoicing at the prospect of having their temple rebuilt, "many of the priests and Levites and heads of the fathers' houses, old men who had seen the first temple, wept with a loud voice when the foundation of this temple was laid" (Ezra 3:12). It was evident that the rebuilt temple would not compare in splendor to Solomon's beautiful sanctuary. But rehearsing these concerns had a depressing influence on the people and weakened the hands of the builders. There were others when the foundation was laid who shouted for joy at what God was doing. The Lord was quick to send an answer to Zerubbabel, again through Haggai, reminding him to be strong in the face of this new problem. He encouraged him with this promise: " ' "I will shake all nations, and they shall come to the Desire of All Nations, and I will fill this temple with glory. . . . The glory of this latter temple shall be greater than the former," says the LORD' " (Haggai 2:7, 9).

What a promise! The question was, How would it be fulfilled? How could this temple possibly be more glorious than Solomon's magnificent temple? It would not be as large or as imposing; it would have no Shekinah glory above the mercy seat, reminding them of God's presence. But God wanted His people to learn through this second chance that the magnificence of a house of worship is not nearly as important as a spirit of humility and contrition in those who worship there! Yet, the question must be answered: why did Haggai declare that this temple would be more glorious than Solomon's? Some five hundred years later, God would send His own Son to give the world a second chance to have life through Him. Would He come as a conquering king, a great religious leader, or as a glorious angel? No, He would come as a humble peasant from the carpenter's shop, without fanfare or impressive credentials! Yet He would come with a glory far greater than Solomon's temple, a glory His people were not prepared to accept.

One day, early in His ministry, Jesus came to His temple only to find money changers cheating the people, demanding outrageous prices for the sacrificial animals being sold for *worship.* What a disappointment it must have been to Jesus, the Son of God, to find His temple, the place where spiritual worship of God should have been taking place, being used instead for merchandising and the disgraceful trafficking of so-called religion. He could have zapped the whole crowd with one brilliant flash of His glory. Instead, He "made a whip of cords . . . [and] drove them all out of the temple. . . . Then His disciples remembered that it was written, 'Zeal for Your house has eaten Me up' " (John 2:15, 17). There was a painful silence, a sense of awe, at the authority of this humble Galilean. Suddenly, "they behold divinity flash through the garb of humanity. The Majesty of heaven stands as the Judge will stand at the last day . . . with the same power to read the soul."[6] The Desire of All Nations had come and filled the temple with His glory! A second chance awaits those who respond!

Let's return to the building of Zerubbabel's temple. The mountains of difficulty that faced the builders helped strengthen their faith. The prophet Zechariah saw a vision of two olive trees standing before God, representing through their oil the presence of the Holy Spirit of God, which He delights to impart to His people who are doing His work. Sometime later, Zechariah was given a vision of an angel who talked with him and encouraged him with these words: " ' "Not by might nor by power, but by my Spirit," says the LORD of hosts' " (Zechariah 4:6). Only God's Spirit can give true second chances! "God's way is to make the day of small things the beginning of the glorious triumph of truth and righteousness."[7]

Thank God for the gift of prophecy and that now in these last days He has again sent a message for His people to build His spiritual temple, a remnant of believers preparing the world for His second coming—not by might or power, but by His Spirit.

Reforms of Ezra and Nehemiah

Both of these men lived and worked during the reign of Artaxerxes, the Medo-Persian ruler who issued the third and final decree for the restoration of Jerusalem. Nehemiah led in completing the building of the walls in Jerusalem, and both men were instrumental in the reorganization of the temple services and were active in leading out in revival and reformation during this time of restoration. We will notice a few examples.

On one occasion the people gathered together "in the open square that was in front of the Water Gate from morning until midday" (Nehemiah 8:3), while Ezra read to them from the book of the Law. Others joined in, "read distinctly" and "helped them to understand the reading" (verse 8). The congregation responded with bowed heads and "worshiped the LORD" (verse 6). They kept the Day of Atonement and later celebrated the Feast of Tabernacles, making booths and sitting under them and listening to the reading of the Law. There was a renewal of the covenant—a rededication of their lives to God!

The renewal of the covenant had implications—reforms that needed to be made. Heathen Tobiah was driven from his room in the court of God's house (see Nehemiah 13:3–9). Nehemiah contended with those who had become entangled in mixed marriages (see Nehemiah 10:28–30; 13:23–29). Sabbath reforms were initiated. The people were treading winepresses on the Sabbath, bringing in their sheaves, and carrying on their usual work. Nehemiah instructed them not to buy wares from the heathen stationed outside the gates on the Sabbath (see Nehemiah 10:31). Heathen influences had led the people of Judah to desecrate the Sabbath by carrying on business as usual on His day. Distressed at the blatant Sabbath breaking, Nehemiah warned the people that it was the profaning of the Sabbath that had brought disaster upon the nation.

In our day, the Sabbath is desecrated by the majority of the Christian world, as well as by some professing Sabbath keepers. Reformation is needed. The greater the evil in our world today, the more urgent it becomes that God's last-day people be reformers in every area of God's covenant commandments, including the holy Sabbath, His day of rest and worship. Those who give God's last message to the world need the Sabbath experience to share with lost people who desperately need one more chance to respond to God's last call to a second chance for life!

---

1. White, *Prophets and Kings,* 512.
2. Sherman A. Nagel, *Cyrus the Persian* (Miami: Pioneer Valley Publishers, 1996).
3. White, *Prophets and Kings,* 557.
4. Ibid., 557, 558.
5. Ibid., 645.
6. White, *The Desire of Ages,* 158.
7. White, *Prophets and Kings,* 595.

CHAPTER 11

Jesus and Glimpses of Glory

There was no room in John's life for religion, but he reluctantly tolerated his wife and children attending church. One cold, snowy evening when they had gone to church, he watched the blowing snow and noticed a flock of wild geese grounded by the wind and desperately looking for shelter near his house. His heart was touched by their dilemma. He tried to direct them to his barn, out of the cold wind, but to no avail. "Why, why, can't I help them? They don't understand. If only I could turn myself into a goose for a few minutes, I could lead the flock to shelter and safety!"

Suddenly, a light turned on in his head—as bright as the falling snow and as warm as the embers by the fireplace. His resistant conscience was smitten! *That's what Jesus did! He, God, became a human being so that He could lead humans out of the storm into safety! Why has it taken me so long to see it?* He fell to his knees, his heart broken by this new insight. What joy that family experienced together that night!

A new kind of glory

As we have already noted, God revealed Himself in His brilliant glory to Moses, Isaiah, and others in Old Testament times. The greatest revelation of His glory came in the form of a tiny bundle born in a stable near Bethlehem. The Messiah had come as a human to lead the "lost geese" to shelter. The shepherds watching their flocks, awed by the heavenly glory, went to find the newborn King. " 'Glory to God in the highest, and on earth peace, goodwill toward men,' " sang the angels (Luke 2:14). Yet the glory of the angelic host that night was surpassed by this unprecedented and glorious event: "the glory shining in the face of Jesus . . . the glory of [His] self-sacrificing love. . . . [Through Christ], Heaven is enshrined in humanity, and humanity is enfolded in the bosom of Infinite Love."[1] Throughout eternity the redeemed will study and wonder at the incomprehensible love shown when God manifested His glory by sending His own Son, hiding His visible glory in a human body so that He might minister to fallen human beings!

How can any human mind wrap itself around that truth? God the Son, the God of the Shekinah glory, humbled Himself to live in the womb of a woman for nine months, in order to become Immanuel, God with us—"God's thought made audible."[2]

Yet, tragically, even the religious leaders of His own people, including most of the priests, did not recognize the Messiah's glory. Humble shepherds and wise men from the East came to worship Him, so why could not His own professed people also see His glory? Had they become so familiar with the forms of worship pointing forward to His coming that their eyes were blinded to their meaning? Had they become so corrupted by power and their own self-importance that His humility was a threat to their pride? Had they become so obsessed with a Messiah who would deliver them from Roman oppression that they rejected the Messiah who had come to deliver them from the bondage of their sinful natures? Was His connection with His Father so powerful that they hated the very glory that they should have welcomed and worshiped? Finally, what can we learn from their mistakes, and how can we prepare our hearts to see the true glory of this wonderful Jesus so that we may worship Him as He deserves?

In this chapter we shall look at snapshots—mere glimpses—of the glory of God as it was revealed in the face and life of Jesus Christ as He walked this earth two thousand years ago.

His baptism and temptation

Though John the Baptist and Jesus were cousins, they had never met. Imagine the anticipation both of them must have felt as they approached their divine appointment. John sensed in Jesus the very atmosphere of divinity. When Jesus requested baptism, John was reluctant, but Jesus assured him that this was necessary to " 'fulfill all righteousness' " (Matthew 3:15). Jesus did not need to be baptized, for He was the Sinless One. Yet, as man's Substitute and Representative, He must be baptized as an example for every believer.

At His baptism, Jesus poured out His soul in prayer. He prayed for His followers; He prayed for Himself. Suddenly, as He came up out of the water, a dovelike form descended on Him. Glorious beams of light, direct from the Father's throne, bathed His countenance, as a voice from heaven declared, " 'This is My beloved Son, in whom I am well pleased' " (verse 17).

As the Son of Man, Jesus must now experience what every human being faces—the power of temptation to sin. He did not place Himself in the path of temptation, but for our sakes He must meet and overcome it! Led into the wilderness by the Holy Spirit, Jesus spent forty days fasting and praying, preparing for the terrible onslaught of the one who, since the Fall, had hoped to usurp His place. Jesus took our nature, so it was possible for Him to yield to temptation. Now the tempter came to Him and suggested that Jesus turn the stones into bread to break His fast. For us, "He exercised a self-control stronger than hunger or death."[3] Jesus would not presume to work a miracle to prove that He was the Son of God. The final temptation was an invitation for Jesus to worship Satan. Christ's answer was prompt and decisive: " ' "You shall worship the LORD your God, and Him only you shall serve" ' " (Matthew 4:10). "Divinity flashed through suffering humanity. . . . Christ's victory was as complete as had been the failure of Adam."[4]

Jesus' glory shone through His victory during that terrible ordeal, and it is our assurance that we, too, can be victorious in the battles of life. Whom we will worship is still an issue we face today. Only through God's grace and power can we resist the temptations to worship the many gods of our society, which constantly confront and demand our allegiance and worship.

"Come and see"

When John the Baptist saw Jesus in the crowd, he cried out, " 'Behold! The Lamb of God!' " (John 1:29). From that time some of John's disciples began to follow Jesus. Andrew and John were the first to respond to the Spirit's call. Andrew called his brother Simon Peter, saying, " 'We have found the Messiah' " (verse 41). Then Jesus called Philip, and Philip, in turn, told Nathaniel. When Nathaniel expressed doubts, Philip urged him, " 'Come and see' " (verse 46). He did, and when he met Jesus, Nathaniel cried out, " 'You are the Son of God! You are the King of Israel!' " (verse 49). Jesus' response was, " 'Hereafter you shall see heaven open, and the angels of God ascending and descending upon the Son of Man' " (verse 51).

What was it that attracted these disciples to Jesus? He offered them no positions of power, no salary—only self-sacrifice, poverty, and even persecution. " 'If anyone desires to come after Me, let him deny himself, and take up his cross daily, and follow Me. For whoever desires to save his life will lose it, but whoever loses his life for My sake will save it' " (Luke 9:23, 24). Jesus was telling His new disciples that in spite of hardships, if they would believe in Him as the Son of God, they would see the heavens opened, never to be closed, and they would see angels bringing blessings from heaven with hope, courage, and help for the children of men.[5]

Jesus: The meaning of true worship

The teachings of Jesus shine with His glory. He taught that prayer was conversation with the Father in heaven, not mere repetitions to impress others. He taught that deeds of charity should be done quietly, not to make one look good, but to help those in need (see Matthew 6:1–4). Jesus repeatedly healed on the Sabbath day to emphasize that it was more important—more in tune with true Sabbath keeping—to heal someone who had been bound for years by a disease than to loose one's animals on the Sabbath so that they could drink water (see Luke 13:11–16).

Jesus' glory shone through His night interview with Nicodemus, a ruler of the Jews, who came secretly to learn more about this new Teacher. Jesus ignored his intended compliment and went right to the heart of the matter! " 'Unless one is born again, he cannot see the kingdom of God' " (John 3:3). In answer to Nicodemus's objection, Jesus made His point very clear: " 'I assure you, no one can enter the Kingdom of God without being born of water and the Spirit. Humans can reproduce only human life, but the Holy Spirit gives birth to spiritual life' " (verses 5, 6, NLT).

Every concept and every word Jesus spoke shines with heaven's light! Nowhere is His divine insight more glorious and succinct than in His brief statement on worship to the Samaritan woman at Jacob's well. Jesus knew human nature. He knew that sinful, fallen humans crave affirmation. Sometimes they seek it through religiosity without thinking of changing their basic human tendencies. They think, *Just wear the forms of religion, follow the accepted customs, make a good show in public, and impress the crowd with piety!* So when the Samaritan woman asked Jesus a very political question—"Where should we worship? Here on this mountain or in Jerusalem?"—He was ready with an answer. " 'The hour is coming,' " He replied to her, " 'when you will neither on this mountain, nor in Jerusalem, worship the Father' " (John 4:21). " 'True worshipers will worship the Father in spirit and truth; for the Father is seeking such to worship Him' " (verse 23).

God Himself gave forms, rituals, and holy days to His people. However, as we have seen previously, He appealed to them again and again through the prophets that form is not enough, even when those forms are carried out according to His instructions. What God really wants is the heart, a heart that responds to Him in humility and in obedience. He desires a heart and a mind that come to Him in a spirit of love and adoration, desiring nothing more than His presence and Spirit. Coming to God, willing to be nothing so that He can be all, a heart touched by His love and compassion—that is worshiping in *spirit.* Worshiping in *truth* means obeying the forms of religion, *because* we have the right *spirit.* That is the worship that God desires and accepts. Yet, how many today still cling to their forms and ceremonies, thinking that these forms of worship will somehow earn them a right to God's kingdom without a heart that is yielded to Him?

Jesus' glory in His miracles

Jesus had just stilled a storm on Galilee. His disciples were overwhelmed at the thought that " 'He commands even the winds and water, and they obey Him!' " (Luke 8:25). As they approached the country of the Gadarenes, they were appalled by a demon-possessed man coming toward them. The demon in the poor wretch cried out to Jesus, " 'What have I to do with You, Jesus, Son of the Most High God? I beg You, do not torment me!' " (verse 28). Jesus allowed the legion of demons to enter a herd of swine, which they did, causing the pigs to "[run] violently down the steep place into the lake and [drown]" (verse 33). Those who witnessed this miracle should have seen the glory of God in the scene that met their eyes as they found the man "sitting at the feet of Jesus, clothed and in his right mind" (verse 35). They missed the point, because their faith was too small! The community asked Jesus to leave, because their temporal interests were greater than their spiritual vision! The healed man begged to be allowed to follow Jesus, but instead, Jesus encouraged him to go home and tell his friends what great things God had done for him (see verse 39).

Sinners and Jesus' glory

Perhaps Jesus' glory shines the brightest in His relationship to sinners. Simon had invited Him to a feast where a woman of ill repute brought a flask of fragrant oil and anointed His feet, weeping tears of repentance and joy at the forgiveness and a new opportunity at life that He had given her. Jesus read the thoughts of His host, Simon, who was muttering to himself that if Jesus were really a prophet, He would know what kind of woman she was and wouldn't let her touch Him (see Luke 7:39)! Jesus told Simon a little parable that got right to the heart of the matter: Two debtors, He said, owed a creditor, one a small amount, the other a much larger amount. The creditor freely forgave them both. Which debtor, Jesus asked, would love him most?

Reluctantly, Simon admitted that the debtor who had been forgiven most would no doubt love him most. Jesus' answer to Simon shines with the glory of God's wonderful grace: " 'Her sins, which are many, are forgiven, for she loved much. But to whom little is forgiven, the same loves little' " (verse 47).

Transfiguration glory

Jesus' earthly ministry was fast drawing to a climax for which His followers were not prepared. One day He took them to Caesarea Philippi, beyond Galilee. They stood at the foot of a hill, where even today one may see the ancient rock where people worshiped a false god. Idolatry was prevalent. Jesus wanted to teach His followers that these people needed to be reached. First, however, the faith of His own disciples must be firm. " 'Who do men say that I . . . am?' " Jesus asked them (Matthew 16:13). His own people had failed to recognize Him as the Messiah. Then Jesus probed a bit deeper. " 'But who do you say that I am?' " (verse 15).

Peter answered without hesitation, " 'You are the Christ, the Son of the living God' " (verse 16). There by that rock where the heathen worshiped, Jesus declared to the disciples that He is the Rock, and that upon Him would be founded the Christian church. Jesus knew their faith would be tested. He desired to strengthen them for what lay ahead. He earnestly prayed for them and tried to help them see that suffering lay ahead for Him. However, a suffering Messiah was not on their agenda! How could He prepare them to see Him die, without losing their faith?

A few days after this encounter, Jesus took His three closest disciples—Peter, James, and John—up to a high mountain. The record says simply, "He was transfigured before them. His face shone like the sun, and His clothes became as white as the light" (Matthew 17:2). Suddenly, Moses and Elijah appeared and talked with Him. Then a brilliant cloud hovered over them, and a voice from the cloud proclaimed, " 'This is My beloved Son, in whom I am well pleased' " (verse 5). The disciples fell on their faces in fear, but Jesus touched them and assured them of His presence. The record says that when they looked up, "they saw no one but Jesus only" (verse 8). It is wonderful to be able to see the glory of God visibly, but His touch was even more important to those disciples that day (see verse 7). They would never forget that touch of their Master and the scene of His glory.

Behold your King is coming

Jesus repeatedly told his disciples about His coming death, but they were in total denial. In fact, it was the triumphal entry that confirmed in their minds that Jesus indeed would set up His kingdom here and now!

Why, then, did Jesus allow this pompous entry into Jerusalem, riding on a donkey like the Israelite kings of old? He had never before permitted any demonstration calling attention to Himself.

The time had come, and the prophecy must be fulfilled. People were already assembling at Jerusalem for the Passover feast. Their attention must be directed to the real Passover Lamb, because He would soon be led to the slaughter—a cruel Roman cross. Never had such a triumphal entry been witnessed. The kings of earth usually had captives in their processions as trophies of their valor—trains of mourners. But Jesus' "captives" were rejoicing in their newfound freedom in this Messiah!

Leading the donkey on which Jesus rode was Lazarus, whom He had raised from the dead.[6] The crowds following Him into Jerusalem swelled! The excitement and anticipation of the people was the worship of happy hearts, hearts that were weary of formality and cold austerity, hearts that longed for a Messiah who would deliver them from the emptiness they experienced.

The glory of that triumphal entry must have lived on in the hearts of those disciples and Jesus' other followers. Through their coming disappointment, it must have somehow given them a ray of hope that this Jesus would eventually reign as the promised King! This hint of future glory was the fire that burned in their hearts and was the source of the growth and spread of early Christianity.

One of the most poignant glimpses of glory in the life of Jesus is recorded by John, as Jesus lifts His eyes to heaven and prays passionately to the Father: " 'Glorify Your Son, that Your Son also may glorify You. . . . And now, O Father, glorify Me . . . with the glory which I had with You before the world was' " (John 17:1, 5). His disciples needed that assurance of His glory! His prayer would linger in their hearts. It would give them courage when all looked dark and dismal. They must catch this glimpse of His glory! What a compassionate and wonderful Savior He is!

Scenes of final glory

The last week of Christ's life was filled with snapshots of His glory, glory that was not always apparent. The glory of the omnipotent God was shown in allowing Himself to be tried before cruel and ungodly judges, though He never gave them an unkind word or look. The glory was there in a Man who was God, but who submitted to the cruelest and most demeaning treatment and still had room in His heart of compassion for a dying, repentant thief. The glory flashed forth in the words He cried out in His dying agony: " 'Father, forgive them, for they do not know what they do' " (Luke 23:34). He who appeared to have been conquered is the Conqueror! As the loud cry, " 'It is finished!' " (John 19:30), escaped His lips, the veil in the temple tore from top to bottom, and the knife in the hand of the ministering priest dropped to the floor. The lamb that was to be sacrificed escaped! The blood of the Passover Lamb was shed! Darkness marked His death, and a great earthquake told the world that this was no ordinary Man. For, even nature mourned when its Creator died!

Jesus was buried. His friends and followers mourned, too. Just as He had rested at the close of Creation week, so now at the close of His earthly work, He rested during the hours of the Sabbath. Though evil angels and Roman soldiers guarded His tomb, no power of evil could keep Him in the grave. When the time came, marked again by an earthquake, Christ came forth from the tomb glorified. His followers went from unbelief to doubt—and finally to rapturous joy![7]

When He appeared on the road to Emmaus to some of His mourning followers, they did not recognize Him. Later, when they realized it was their Master, they cried out, " 'Did not our heart burn within us while He talked with us on the road?' " (Luke 24:32). The glory factor comes wrapped in different packages, but always it has the same effect on hearts that are open to the Holy Spirit!

There are other glimpses of glory in those last days of His earthly journey, but the last earthly manifestation of His glory was much like the next one that the human family will witness at His return to this earth. "Now when He had spoken these things, while they watched, He was taken up, and a cloud received Him out of their sight. And while they looked steadfastly toward heaven as He went up, behold, two men stood by them in white apparel, who also said, 'Men of Galilee, why do you stand gazing up into heaven? This same Jesus, who was taken up from you into heaven, will so come in like manner as you saw Him go into heaven' " (Acts 1:9–11).

"Even so, come, Lord Jesus!" (Revelation 22:20).

---

1. White, *The Desire of Ages,* 20, 26.
2. Ibid., 19.
3. Ibid., 117.
4. Ibid., 130.
5. See ibid., 142, 143.
6. Ibid., 572.
7. See ibid., 780.

CHAPTER 12

Worship and the Early Church

On Passover night, when Jesus had finished His Last Supper with His disciples, He predicted that Peter would deny Him. Peter protested, "Though all men shall be offended because of thee, yet will I never be offended" (Matthew 26:33, KJV). How little Peter knew the weakness of his own good intentions. His self-confidence was stronger than his ability to resist the scorn of those who questioned his relationship to Jesus (see verses 69–75)!

Now, only a few weeks later, Peter and his fellow disciples are changed men. Their sorrow and confusion have been transformed into an attitude of joy and a hopeful sense of triumph, because, though the living Christ is no longer with them in person, they sense His presence, the presence of His own Holy Spirit. Their confidence is in Him; Jesus is their badge of authority and the source of their success. How can they fail with Him living in their hearts? No matter what they may face—trials, persecution, even death—their fear is gone, replaced by their confidence in the One who died and is now risen and in heaven, interceding for them!

Day by day, they pray for the heavenly unction of the Holy Spirit to fill their lives and fit them for the work of winning souls for Christ's kingdom.

"When the Day of Pentecost had fully come, they were all with one accord in one place. And suddenly there came a sound from heaven, as of a rushing mighty wind, and it filled the whole house where they were sitting. Then there appeared to them divided tongues, as of fire, and one sat upon each of them.

And they were all filled with the Holy Spirit and began to speak with other tongues, as the Spirit gave them utterance" (Acts 2:1–4).

Peter's Pentecost sermon

Peter stood boldly before the crowd, addressing people from many nations and languages, and all understood him in their own language. His scripture text was from the Old Testament prophet Joel. " ' "And it shall come to pass in the last days, says God, that I will pour out of My Spirit on all flesh; your sons and your daughters shall prophesy, your young men shall see visions, your old men shall dream dreams. And on My menservants and on My maidservants I will pour out My Spirit in those days; and they shall prophesy. . . . And it shall come to pass that whoever calls on the name of the LORD shall be saved" ' " (Acts 2:17, 18, 21).

Peter also quoted Psalm 16:8–11, showing that David predicted the coming of the Holy One, whom Peter declared to be Jesus of Nazareth (Acts 2:22–28). " 'Therefore,' " he continued, " 'let all the house of Israel know assuredly that God has made this Jesus, whom you crucified, both Lord and Christ' " (verse 36). His sermon touched a chord in many hearts, " 'Men and brethren,' " they asked, " 'what shall we do?' " (verse 37). Peter's instant response was, " 'Repent, and let every one of you be baptized in the name of Jesus Christ . . . and you shall receive the gift of the Holy Spirit' " (verse 38). The result? Three thousand souls were added to the church that day as a result of the Holy Spirit's work on their hearts through Peter's sermon.

What made Peter's sermon so powerful? Not only was it Spirit filled, but it was based on Old Testament scripture, with which his hearers were familiar. It held up Jesus Christ as the divine Son of God and appealed to the listeners to accept Jesus as their Savior, repent of their sins, be baptized, and receive the gift of the Holy Spirit. The early disciples were passionate about their Jesus. They wanted everyone to know that He, indeed, was the Messiah promised by the Old Testament prophets. The results were astounding.

Following his account of Peter's successful sermon, Luke comments on some of the things that made the early church witness so successful:

- The church "continued steadfastly in the apostles' doctrine and fellowship" (verse 42). Notice how these two ideas are linked. Fellowship—meeting together for worship—is important, but it must be linked to correct biblical doctrine.

- The church members practiced breaking bread together (see verse 42). This undoubtedly included both eating together socially for fellowship as well as celebrating the Communion service.
- Their fellowship included having "all things in common" (verse 44). That is, they had a common purse to help those in need.
- The regularly met in the temple for worship (see verse 46). The Jewish temple was still recognized as the place of worship by these early believers.
- They went from house to house, eating together, praising the Lord, and witnessing to their faith in Jesus (see verses 46, 47).
- They found favor with the people, no doubt, through visiting and encouraging them in their homes (see verse 47).
- Because of their faithfulness, "the Lord added to the church daily those who were being saved" (verse 47). Sometimes converts to the faith drift away from the church about as fast as they come into the church. Could the key to remaining faithful be that it must be *the Lord* who adds converts to the church? Through human instruments to be sure, but the Lord must do the converting, rather than the human agent doing the converting!
- Many signs and wonders were done through the apostles. Acts 3 records the healing of a lame man, who had lain at the temple gate, asking for alms from the worshipers. When John and Peter saw him, they were quick to tell him that they had no silver or gold to give him, but something much better. " 'In the name of Jesus Christ . . . rise up and walk' " (Acts 3:6). Imagine the impact of this miracle on those coming to worship at the temple. They had seen this poor, lame man lying there for years, begging alms. Now in an instant he was healed! "They were filled with wonder" (verse 10).

Peter waxed bold when he was brought before the religious leaders. He accused them of murdering Jesus " 'whom God raised from the dead' " (Acts 4:10). Peter ended his appeal to these leaders by quoting Psalm 118:22: " 'This is the "stone which was rejected by you builders, which has become the chief cornerstone." Nor is there salvation in any other, for there is no other name under heaven given among men by which we must be saved' " (verses 11, 12). What holy boldness, what power in these men who "had been with Jesus" (verse 13). No amount of threatening could stop their witness. They insisted, " 'We cannot but speak the things which we have seen and heard' " (verse 20).

When they had been released, they sang together a song of David (Psalm 2:1, 2). " ' "Why did the nations rage, and the people plot vain things? The kings of the earth took their stand, and the rulers were gathered together against the LORD and against His Christ" ' " (verse 25, 26). Once again, as they met and prayed together, the Holy Spirit was poured out on this meeting of His servants and "they spoke the word of God with boldness" (verse 31).

As the apostles continued to work miracles and to preach in Jerusalem, the high priest was angered, for they were influencing the people. He had the apostles imprisoned, but not for long. An angel of the Lord delivered them. Imagine the consternation of the high priest to learn that these men were again teaching in the temple! The calm answer of Peter and the other apostles to the frustrated high priest, was simply, " 'We ought to obey God rather than men' " (Acts 5:29)! Gamaliel, a teacher of law, reminded the leaders, " 'If . . . this work is of men, it will come to nothing; but if it is of God, you cannot overthrow it—lest you even be found to fight against God' " (verses 38, 39).

Stephen's sermon and martyrdom

As the work progressed, the need arose for more organized help. Seven deacons were chosen to assist in the work of making sure that the widows and the poor were cared for, thus freeing the apostles for the work of preaching. The record also notes that "a great many of the priests were obedient to the faith" (Acts 6:7).

Stephen, one of the seven deacons, was a man of faith and did many mighty works and miracles among the people (see verse 8). So powerful was his witness that the council called him to give an account; they hired false witnesses to testify against him.

Stephen's defense turned into a sermon to the council (see Acts 7). He began by recounting God's call to Abraham and God's leading in Abraham's life and in the lives of his descendants. Then he spoke words that infuriated the crowd, though he must have spoken them with pathos and love: " 'You stiff-necked and uncircumcised in heart and ears! You always resist the Holy Spirit; as your fathers did, so do you' " (verse 51). He accused them of murdering the " 'Just One' " (verse 52).

That was too much for them! "They were cut to the heart, and they gnashed at him with their teeth" (verse 54). Stephen's sermon ended abruptly. The record says that as he gazed up into heaven he saw "Jesus standing at the right hand of God" (verse 55). A mob mentality took over the crowd. They took Stephen outside the city and stoned him to death "as he was calling on God and saying, 'Lord Jesus receive my spirit' " (verse 59). He prayed for God to forgive their blindness and sin, and "when he had said this, he fell asleep" (verse 60).

Saul, from persecutor to evangelist

The record says simply that "Saul was consenting to his [Stephen's] death" (Acts 8:1). There was a great persecution of the church, with Saul making "havoc of the church" (verse 3). He dragged Christian believers to prison, caring not if they were men or women. Was this man angry at the church? Or was he under the conviction of the Holy Spirit?

The story of Saul's conversion is recorded in Acts 9. On the road to Damascus to hunt down more Christians and bring them bound back to Jerusalem, this man had murder in his heart! Suddenly, he saw a bright light shining from heaven and heard a Voice: " 'Saul, Saul, why are you persecuting Me?' " (verse 4). Imagine his shock when he heard that Voice say, " 'I am Jesus, whom you are persecuting. It is hard for you to kick against the goads' " (verse 5).

" 'Lord, what do You want me to do?' " Saul asked (verse 6). That's the question the Lord is waiting to hear from all the "Sauls" out there!

Power, passion, and purpose

The *power* of these early apostles and church leaders came from their infilling by the Holy Spirit. Another example is that of Philip, one of the seven deacons. On his way from Jerusalem to Gaza, through the desert, he met a eunuch, a man of authority under Candace, the queen of Ethiopia. Hearing this man reading from Isaiah and impressed by the Spirit, Philip asked him, " 'Do you understand what you are reading?' " (Acts 8:30) That was the opening of a Bible study from the book of Isaiah that led to an almost immediate baptism (see Acts 8:26–39)!

Another example involves Cornelius, a Roman centurion and "a devout man . . . who feared God . . . who gave alms generously . . . and [who] prayed to God" (Acts 10:2). One day as he was praying, an angel appeared to him in vision, called him by name, and assured him that his prayers had come up before God. He was instructed where to go to find Simon Peter, who would instruct him what to do. However, first God must change Peter's anti-Gentile mind-set. So He gave Peter a vision of a sheet let down from heaven that was filled with all kinds of animals (see Acts 10:9–16). The Lord instructed him, " 'Rise Peter; kill and eat' " (verse 13).

"Oh no, Lord. I've never eaten unclean animals!" Peter responded. Later, when Peter was explaining to Cornelius why he had come to preach to Gentiles, he said that in this vision " 'God has shown me that I should not call any man common or unclean' " (verse 28).

The gospel now spread to the Gentiles. They were converted, and the Holy Spirit fell on them as well as on the Jewish Christians. God is no respecter of persons. He is the Creator of the human family, and He wants both Jews and Gentiles to be in His kingdom. The Holy Spirit is not limited to any race or nationality. His power is available to everyone who chooses Him.

The *passion* of these early disciples and church leaders was for the Lord Jesus Christ, their Savior. That passion motivated them to witness and share, regardless of the cost to themselves—imprisonment or even death, it mattered not. For them, all that counted was that they preach this wonderful Jesus, who died, arose, and now ministered in heaven in their behalf.

As Christians in these last days of earth's history, we would do well to ask ourselves, What is my passion quotient for Jesus? How long has it been since I sacrificed something really important for Him? When have I gone out of my way to witness for Him to someone who really needed to hear the good news? What does my daily life say about my passion for Jesus?

About this time, wicked King Herod had James, the brother of John, killed with the sword (see Acts 12:1, 2). Seeing how much this pleased the Jews, he proceeded to put Peter in prison near the time of the Passover feast. He made sure that Peter was securely bound in chains between two soldiers. In the middle of the night "an angel of the Lord stood by him [Peter], and a light shone in the prison" (Acts 12:7). Peter's chains fell off, and the angel told him to dress himself and come with him. Peter thought he was dreaming. They passed the prison guards and went through the prison's iron gate. Finally, when they came to the house of John Mark's mother, Peter realized that he was not dreaming. This was a for-real deliverance!

No matter how the early Christians witnessed through the Holy Spirit's power, no matter how their passion for Jesus was demonstrated, no matter how they fulfilled their purpose to share the gospel with both Jews and Gentiles, the work went forward and God's name was honored and Jesus was glorified! The worship life of the early church was vibrant and alive. Jesus was real to them, for they had witnessed His presence with them. They were on fire for their wonderful Lord and Master.

The preaching of the apostles

We turn now to another important aspect of the early church's success in giving the gospel to the world of their day. The book of Acts records at least parts of a dozen sermons preached by Peter, Steven, Philip, and Paul, who at first was known as Saul. A brief look at Paul's sermons will demonstrate not only their importance to the success of the work but will emphasize and highlight preaching as an important part of the worship life of the church.

Almost immediately after appearing to Saul on the road to Damascus, the Lord spoke to Ananias in a vision and instructed him to go visit him (see Acts 9:11). Ananias protested, but the Lord assured him that Saul " 'is a chosen vessel of Mine to bear My name before Gentiles, kings, and the children of Israel' " (verse 15). Obediently, Ananias went to see "Brother Saul" and laid hands on him and prayed that he might be filled with the Holy Spirit. At once, scales fell from Saul's eyes; "he received his sight . . . and he arose and was baptized" (verse 18). "Immediately he preached the Christ in the synagogues, that He is the Son of God" (verse 20). The people were amazed; the Jews were confounded and plotted to kill Saul. Even some of the disciples were distrustful of Saul's conversion, but Barnabas brought him to the apostles. Saul shared with them his conversion experience, and they were convinced as they heard his powerful testimony!

The Holy Spirit gave directions that Paul should work with Barnabas, who would nurture and train him for ministry. As they came to Antioch in Pisidia, they went to the synagogue where Paul preached his first Sabbath sermon. He addressed the Jews, reviewing the history of his people from the time they left Egypt, through their wilderness wandering, their settlement in the Promised Land, and the period of the judges and the kings. He spoke of David, a man after God's own heart, saying, " 'From this man's seed . . . God raised up for Israel a Savior—Jesus' " (Acts 13:23). Paul closed his sermon with a passionate appeal to the children of Abraham: " 'We declare to you glad tidings—that promise which was made to the fathers. God has fulfilled this for us their children, in that He has raised up Jesus' " (verses 32, 33).

The next Sabbath Paul preached again, and the whole city came out to hear him. The Jews became upset and began to argue with Paul and his teaching. In boldness, he told them that by rejecting the message of Jesus they were proving themselves unworthy of everlasting life. " 'Behold,' " he said, " 'we turn to the Gentiles' " (verse 46).

Acts 24 tells what happened when Paul was brought before Felix, the governor of Caesarea. He defended himself before Felix by telling how he had come to Jerusalem to worship at the temple and had been arrested on the basis of false accusations. " 'But this I confess to you,' " he said, " 'that according to the Way which they call a sect, so I worship the God of my fathers, believing all things which are written in the Law and the Prophets' " (Acts 24:14). Later, Paul was again called before Felix and his Jewish wife Drusilla to speak of his faith in Christ. "Now as he [Paul] reasoned about righteousness, self-control, and the judgment to come, Felix was afraid and answered, 'Go away for now; when I have a convenient time I will call for you' " (verse 25). Notice how boldly Paul spoke to those who knew and understood the Old Testament prophecies.

There are three ways to respond to straight preaching: repentance, procrastination, or rejection. Both of the latter are dangerous and unacceptable. Yet how many today still refuse to repent, or put it off, hoping that the issue will go away and resolve itself? Straight preaching demands straight thinking and honesty in looking at one's own condition. The preacher cannot control the response to his preaching; he can only be faithful in doing what God commissions!

The questions that every church leader and pastor must ask are

- Do my messages challenge people's comfort zone?
- Is the message truly biblical preaching that will convict hearts?
- Does the message help people see the real issues they are facing?
- Does the message present Christ so attractively that people have a desire to follow Him?

From Felix, Paul was sent to Festus and then later to King Agrippa. Paul's testimony before Agrippa was powerful. " 'Do you believe the prophets?' " he confronted the king. " 'I know that you do believe' " (Acts 26:27).

The king responded, " 'You almost persuade me to become a Christian' " (verse 28). So close, yet so far! How many today come to church and hear God's Word? They know it is true; they know what they should do. They are almost persuaded, but the love of sin in their lives keeps them from making that commitment to the only One who can save them. "Almost persuaded" is not enough! Salvation through Jesus Christ must be an all-or-nothing matter. "Almost saved" means to be totally lost!

We are living in the last days of earth's history, when the enemy of souls is at work to distract every believer from the most important issues of life. Witnessing to those out of Christ, helping them to see their need of salvation, should be our first work. We are to keep our eyes fixed on the cross of Jesus Christ, remembering our own needs and focusing on the needs of others. As we do so, the Holy Spirit will guide us in our witness as He did for those devoted believers in the early church.

"In every true disciple . . . [God's] love, like sacred fire, burns on the altar of the heart. . . . It is on the earth that His children are to reflect this love through blameless lives. Thus sinners will be led to the cross to behold the Lamb of God."[1]

---

1. Ellen G. White, *The Acts of the Apostles* (Mountain View, Calif.: Pacific Press®, 1911), 334.

CHAPTER 13

Worship: From the Mundane to the Sublime

You are a patient in the hospital. Whatever your problem, it is likely that a technician from respiratory therapy will bring you a little gadget to practice breathing deeply, to help you avoid getting pneumonia. You place your lips on the mouthpiece and inhale as best you can; the gauge goes up a bit. You try again and then again. You make some progress but not much. The technician tells you to keep trying—several times a day!

Have you ever felt that your worship experience is like blowing on that little respiratory gadget? You try hard to bring something to God for worship, but sometimes it seems that your efforts go about as high as your feeble attempts to blow in the gadget! Now consider another scenario.

Finding the sublime

A friend has invited you to attend a performance of Handel's *Messiah,* to be given in a lovely cathedral. There is a sense of expectancy in the air as you arrive. The orchestra is tuning up, and soon the choir members take their places. Two hours of magnificent music go by quickly as you sit enthralled by what is perhaps one of the greatest works of art in all of human history. Then comes that thrilling moment when the orchestra begins the moving strains of the grand "Hallelujah" chorus. The audience stands to its feet as one person. You stand tall, at times afraid to breathe for fear of breaking the wonder of the moment. You close your eyes, for you feel you are being drawn closer to heaven than you've ever been before! As the last glorious strains die out, you dread the applause that interrupts the solemnity of the moment. You have worshiped; you have experienced a sublime worship of your Savior you hardly thought possible from your poor human frame. You want to hold on to the moment and never let it die in your heart. If this is what heavenly worship is like you don't want to miss it! Neither do I!

Patmos

Through the years, the beloved apostle John had come to understand the meaning of the self-sacrificing love modeled by his beloved Lord. He had seen persecution and witnessed the destruction of his beloved Jerusalem. He had been tried for his faith at Rome, falsely accused, and cast into a cauldron of boiling oil. His enemies decided that if they couldn't boil him to death, they would banish him, thus ending his influence! How wrong they were!

So there John was, alone and isolated on a rocky island in the Aegean Sea. Though surrounded by beauty, John's loneliness and his separation from friends must have given him a feeling of the mundane. But even in his terrible isolation, he found comfort in God's created works.

There in that lonely environment God opened the very windows of heaven, and John the revelator was shown magnificent visions of worship that have inspired believers in Christ through the centuries. These are visions that have been left for all of God's children through the ages, to motivate and encourage us to worship God, no matter what the cost. Visions of worship that give us hope and courage to know that we, too, may someday worship our God around the throne in sublime worship beyond anything we can imagine here below! Yes, we may face trials, suffering, even persecution. But the visions of John the revelator remind us that "the sufferings of this present time are not worthy to be compared with the glory which shall be revealed in us" (Romans 8:18).

John vividly portrays those sufferings through the centuries as a great conflict that rages between good and evil—a conflict over who has the right to our worship! John is shown numerous scenes of worship that we will consider in this chapter. First, let's get the setting in which John describes this conflict between Christ and Satan. He portrays the intensity of the great conflict under the symbol of a dragon trying to destroy a woman who bears a male Child who will rule all nations. John sees the Child caught up to God and the woman persecuted.

He sees the dragon enraged at the woman, spewing out his wrath and making war against her offspring (see Revelation 12).

Finally, John sees a beast rising up out of the sea, receiving its authority from a dragon, and the whole world wonders after this beast. Then another lamblike beast comes up and exercises all the power of the first beast, deceiving the world with signs and lying wonders. Finally, the ultimate death decree goes forth—no one may buy or sell unless they bear the mark of the beast (see Revelation 13).

In chapter 14, John sees a Lamb standing on Mount Zion, and he hears the voices of victory of those who are following the Lamb and who have been redeemed by His blood. In this setting, John utters one of the most urgent messages in the book of Revelation, if not of the whole Bible—a warning against worshiping the beast. On those who ignore this warning and receive the mark of the beast, God's wrath will be poured out in the final destruction of all who refuse to worship the true Creator God of the universe.

We have seen throughout this book that worship is the real issue in the great conflict between good and evil. From the Fall in Genesis to the temptations of our Lord in the wilderness, worship is at the heart of the battle between Christ and Satan. In the book of Revelation, John pictures the course of this war over worship from the Cross to the final great battle when the enemy will be destroyed at last and the whole universe will worship the Father and the Lamb. The final call of a loving Father, who wants to save all of His earthly children, is uttered in urgency and pathos with a loud voice so that no one can miss it. It is an appeal to every human being living on planet Earth: " 'Fear God and give glory to Him, for the hour of His judgment has come; and *worship Him who made heaven and earth, the sea and springs of water*' " (Revelation 14:7; emphasis supplied).

It is as if God is saying in one final plea, "Please listen. I am your Creator God. I made you. I want your love and your worship. I don't want you to be destroyed even though you have chosen to follow and worship the enemy. There is nothing more I can do unless you turn to Me and honor Me with your love and faith. I don't want you to be destroyed, but if you persist in worshiping the beast and receiving its mark, there is nothing more I can do to save you, for the judgments that destroy the enemy will destroy you if you worship him. Oh, please listen and turn to Me before it is too late!" That is the heart cry of a loving Creator God who paid the ultimate price to save His erring human children.

For those who respond to that call, the rewards are beyond comprehension!

Through John, Jesus has given us wonderful glimpses of what worship in eternity will be like! We turn now to those divine worship scenes John was privileged to see occurring around the throne of God in the heavenly sanctuary.

Who is worshiped and who worships?

The very first worship scene appears early in John's book. He is "in the Spirit on the Lord's Day [God's holy Sabbath]" (Revelation 1:10). He looks and sees none other than his blessed Savior. He falls down at His feet and then feels the gentle touch of Jesus' right hand on his shoulder. " 'Do not be afraid; I am the First and the Last. I am He who lives, and was dead, and behold, I am alive forevermore. Amen' " (verses 17, 18). What an assurance to the aged soldier of the cross! This was none other than his beloved Master, Jesus! John is told to write what he sees in a book, so that all Jesus' followers may have the assurance John was given there on that lonely island.

In chapter 4, John is shown "a throne set in heaven, and One sat on the throne. And He . . . was like a jasper and a sardius stone . . . and there was a rainbow around the throne, in appearance like an emerald" (verses 2, 3). Twenty-four elders and four living creatures stand around the throne, singing, " 'Holy, holy, holy, Lord God Almighty, who was and is and is to come' " (verse 8). "The living creatures give glory and honor and thanks to Him who sits on the throne, who lives forever and ever, the twenty-four elders fall down before Him . . . and worship Him . . . and cast their crowns before the throne, saying: 'You are worthy, O Lord, to receive glory and honor and power; for You created all things, and by Your will they exist and were created' " (verses 9–11).

Why God is worshiped

In order to better understand how and why we should worship, let's note again John's descriptions of how heavenly beings and the redeemed worship. The Greek word translated as "worship" in John's descriptions, means to "prostrate oneself in homage," "to reverence," "to adore."[1] In John's first vision of worship, he says, "When I saw Him [the Son of Man], I fell at His feet like a dead man" (Revelation 1:17, NASB). The risen Christ appeared to him in the brilliance of the noonday sun, and John simply fell prostrate to the ground, almost lifeless, so great was Christ's glory!

In the vision of Revelation 5, John sees Christ as the slain Lamb, while the elders and the living creatures sing a new song: " 'You are worthy to take the scroll . . . for You were slain, and have redeemed us to God by Your blood . . . and have made us kings and priests to our God' " (verses 9, 10). God is Creator, Redeemer, Deliverer, King of kings and Lord of lords, and the Judge seated on the great white throne, for He is worthy!

This should be a matter of great concern to those who claim to worship the Creator God of the universe, because so often we come into the place of worship as casually as we might enter a concert hall or a place of entertainment! Do we really have a biblical understanding of the greatness and wonder of the God we claim to worship? Or is worship just a form we go through because it's a habit or the proper thing to do? How can we develop a sense of the awesomeness and glory of our wonderful God? Certainly, an understanding of John's visions of heavenly worship should be a first step in developing a new sense of awe and wonder at the greatness of our God. They should motivate us to worship Him with every fiber of our being and of our love and adoration of Him.

There are several principles here worth noting:

1. God has given us a pattern in Scripture of what worship should look like. The original design for worship is heavenly, and fallen human beings should be very careful not to ignore or replace God's plan with their own ideas about how to worship.
2. God's law and His covenant must be the basis of all true worship. That includes obedience to the first four commandments, which are the very foundation for all true worship.
3. Both the earthly and the heavenly sanctuaries provide a model for how God is to be reverenced and held in awe as we worship Him.
4. John's visions of worship illustrate that God has ordained leaders in worship. The Levite musicians in the Old Testament system were trained ministers who led in the worship music of the sanctuary. In Revelation, the twenty-four elders and the four living creatures appear to lead in the worship of God and the Lamb.
5. True biblical worship, as described in the book of Revelation, is often accompanied by dramatic evidence of God's power, including exalted songs of praise, glory, and honor.
6. As already noted, the meaning of the word *worship* is to prostrate

oneself in humility, reverence, and awe, as a sign of our submission to God's greatness, holiness, and majesty. Worship is the honor we give to our wonderful Creator and Redeemer!

7. In true worship, God alone is honored as the sovereign Ruler of the universe![2]

The vision in Revelation 4 describes the worship scene in a setting of a great display of power, with the four living creatures who do not rest day or night, singing to the Lord: " 'Holy, holy, holy, Lord God Almighty' " (verse 8). Then "the twenty four elders fall down before Him . . . and worship Him . . . and cast their crowns before the throne, saying: 'You are worthy, O Lord, to receive glory and honor and power; for You created all things, and by Your will they exist and were created' " (verses 10, 11). Here, as in many of John's worship visions, the emphasis is on God's worthiness for worship, because He is the Creator and Sustainer of all things. John is simply reiterating here what he declared in his Gospel: "In the beginning was the Word, and the Word was with God, and the Word was God. . . . All things were made through Him, and without Him nothing was made that was made" (John 1:1, 3). And Paul asserts, "For by Him all things were created that are in heaven and that are on earth, visible and invisible. . . . All things were created through Him and for Him. And He is before all things, and in Him all things consist" (Colossians 1:16, 17).

John sees a scroll in the right hand of the One sitting on the throne, and he hears a loud voice saying, " 'Who is worthy to open the scroll and to loose its seals?' " (Revelation 5:2). Again his attention is drawn to the throne with the living creatures and elders surrounding it. Now he sees a Lamb as though it had been slain, who is also " 'the Lion of the tribe of Judah, the Root of David' " (verse 5). Suddenly, all of the creatures and elders fall down before Him, singing a "new song . . . 'You are worthy to take the scroll, and to open its seals; for You were slain, and have redeemed us to God by Your blood . . . and have made us kings and priests to our God; and we shall reign on the earth' " (verses 9, 10). The angelic choirs join their voices in a grand chorus: " 'Worthy is the Lamb who was slain to receive power and riches and wisdom, and strength and honor and glory and blessing' " (verse 12).

What a glorious worship scene! He who was crucified on a cruel cross by religious zealots, He who was crowned with thorns instead of the crown He deserved, is now being worshiped by great multitudes of the redeemed who sing.

Such worship is the highest experience that can come to human beings created in the image of God! According to John's visions, such worship is the ongoing activity of heaven. Our poor, finite minds cannot even begin to grasp the reality and the sublimity of such worship. Yet God wants us to have that experience. Now is our preparation time to learn how to truly worship God in reverence and awe and humility. As we observed earlier, all true worship from human beings must begin with a broken and contrite heart, which has been humbled before a Holy God in repentance of our sinful humanity. Only then can God have permission to change and transform our lives so that we can offer Him acceptable worship!

The example of the worshipers bowing around God's throne in John's visions demonstrates anew that God's very nature and Spirit must be the basis of all worship of Him. Worship is not about us; it is a gift—the best our poor human hearts can give—that we offer to Him as our divine Creator and Maker. It is not about how we feel about worship or what we think God wants or what appeals to us. Worship is a gift we bring to God, based on what He has revealed in His holy Word about Himself, which determines how we come to Him to worship!

In another worship scene (Revelation 14:1–5), John describes the redeemed singing a new song around God's throne, "for they are without fault" (verse 5) and "follow the Lamb wherever He goes" (verse 4). Later, John sees the same group of the redeemed sitting on thrones of judgment (see Revelation 20:4). Some are those who had been beheaded and martyred because they refused to worship the beast or to compromise their faith in the living Christ. All had made the choice to worship only God.

Where is the throne of God?

In John's first worship vision, as noted earlier, he saw the Son of Man walking amid the seven golden candlesticks in the Holy Place of the sanctuary. In Revelation 4:2, John saw "a throne set in heaven." Again, in Revelation 8:3, John saw the throne near the golden altar where much incense was being offered with the prayers of the saints, ascending before God. What a beautiful picture of our Great High Priest and Intercessor offering up His precious blood and righteousness, along with our worship, before the very throne of God! That fact alone is such good news that it should fill our hearts with joy, love, and adoration as we fall before Him to worship and praise Him for what He is doing for us in the heavenly sanctuary, at His very throne!

Revelation 11 pictures a worship scene announcing the coming of Jesus, as His final reign is about to begin. Once more, the twenty-four elders fall on their faces and worship God, thanking Him that He is about to take His rightful place as king of the nations to administer the final judgment of those who refuse His salvation and righteous rule (see verses 15–17). Notice what happens next. "Then the temple of God was opened in heaven, and the *ark of His covenant was seen in His temple.* And there were lightnings, noises, thunderings, an earthquake, and great hail" (verse 19; emphasis supplied).

God's holy law is contained in the ark of the covenant, symbol of both His holy righteousness and His unerring judgment on those who refuse to abide by the principles of His law. Now His final work of reward to the redeemed and judgment on those who have refused His offers of mercy, are about to begin. God's holy law has been exonerated. The wicked stand condemned by the law that they have broken, rejected, and trampled—the law that now condemns them to the second death.

Revelation 15 presents another fascinating worship scene. John saw seven angels about to pour out the wrath of God in the form of seven terrible plagues. The next moment, he saw "a sea of glass mingled with fire" and those who stand there are "those who have the victory over the beast, over his image and over his mark" (verse 2). With their harps and voices, "they sing the song of Moses, the servant of God, and the song of the Lamb, saying: 'Great and marvelous are Your works, Lord God Almighty! Just and true are Your ways, O King of the saints! Who shall not fear You, O Lord, and glorify Your name? For You alone are holy. . . . For Your judgments have been manifested' " (verses 3, 4). As the scene ended, "the temple was filled with smoke from the glory of God and from His power, and no one was able to enter the temple till the seven plagues of the seven angels were completed" (verse 8).

Now John hears a multitude of voices singing a great Alleluia chorus to the Lord our God, because His righteous judgments have prevailed and " 'the great harlot who corrupted the earth' " has been dealt with (Revelation 19:2). Again, the twenty-four elders and the four living creatures worship God around the throne! Then John describes the Holy City, New Jerusalem, coming down from God out of heaven and a loud voice proclaiming that " 'the tabernacle of God is with men, and . . . God Himself will be with them and be their God' " (Revelation 21:3). John saw no temple in the New Jerusalem, "for the Lord God Almighty and the Lamb are its temple" (verse 22). John ends his heavenly visions by reminding us again of God's invitation: "The Spirit and the bride say, 'Come!' " (Revelation 22:17). How can we afford to neglect such an invitation?

No more night

John must have thrilled as he saw the New Jerusalem coming down from God out of heaven. In the city there is no need for a sun or moon, for the Lamb is its light (see Revelation 21:23). "The nations of those who are saved shall walk in its light [the light of the glory of God]" (verse 24). Nothing that defiles can enter there. No more sin, no more pollution, no more oil spills, no earthquakes, no hurricanes or no tsunamis. No more cancer, no more deadly disease, no more germs of any kind. No more sin, no more tragedy or death! God has cleansed and purified the earth of all these and more in the final fires that wipe away every defilement, every abomination, every damnable lie!

Perhaps that is why the psalmist, in his beautiful Sabbath praise song, suddenly interrupts his train of praise and cries out in anticipation, "For behold, Your enemies shall perish; all the workers of iniquity shall be scattered" (Psalm 92:9).

Now John quickly adds another interesting dimension. Almost parenthetically, he mentions that there shall be no night in the holy city. (Perhaps the nights on Patmos were unbearably dark!)

> Gone is the curse from which I stumbled and fell.
> Evil is banished. . . .
> No more night, no more pain,
> No more tears, never crying again.
> Praises to the great I Am;
> We will live in the light of the risen Lamb.[3]

The redeemed bring their glory and honor to their King. They worship Him through all eternity for their names are written in the Lamb's book of life! They have learned to worship Him in their earthly sojourn; now they will spend all eternity in singing praises and worshiping their God and the Lamb.

> Hallelujah! Hallelujah! Hallelujah!
> For the Lord God Omnipotent reigneth . . .
> The kingdoms of this world have become the

Kingdom of our Lord and of His Christ . . .
And He shall reign forever and ever . . .
King of kings, and Lord of lords
And He shall reign forever and ever.
Hallelujah! Hallelujah! Hallelujah![4]

---

1. Spiros Zodhiates, ed., *Hebrew-Greek Key Word Study Bible* (Chattanooga, Tenn.: AMG Publishers, 1991), 4352.

2. Wilson-Bridges, *Levite Praise;* adapted from chapter 1.

3. Walt Harrah, "No More Night" (Nashville: Word Music, 1984).

4. George Frideric Handel, "Hallelujah," in *Messiah,* ed. Watkins Shaw, Novello Handel ed. (London: Novello, 2003).